Thomas Hughes

Memoir of a Brother

Thomas Hughes

Memoir of a Brother

ISBN/EAN: 9783744649537

Printed in Europe, USA, Canada, Australia, Japan

Cover: Foto ©Thomas Meinert / pixelio.de

More available books at **www.hansebooks.com**

MEMOIR OF A BROTHER.

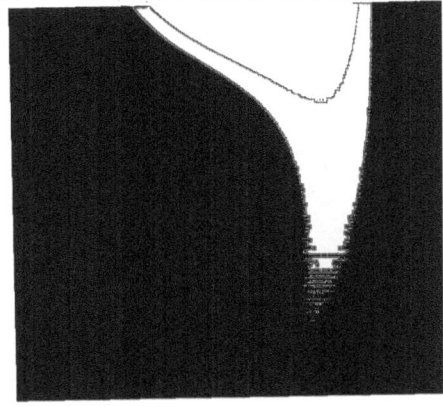

BY

THOMAS HUGHES,

AUTHOR OF "TOM BROWN'S SCHOOLDAYS."

FOURTH EDITION.

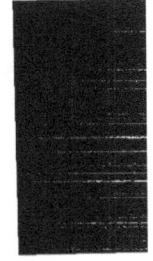

London:

MACMILLAN AND CO.

1873.

LONDON
R. CLAY, SONS, AND TAYLOR, PRINTERS,
BREAD STREET HILL

PREFACE.

This Memoir was written for, and at the request of, the near relatives, and intimate friends, of the home-loving country gentleman, whose unlooked-for death had made them all mourners indeed. Had it been meant originally for publication, it would have taken a very different form. In compiling it, my whole thoughts were fixed on my own sons and nephews, and not on the public. It tells of a life with which indeed the public has no concern in one sense; for my brother, with all his ability and power of different kinds, was one of the humblest and most retiring of men; who just did his own duty, and held his own tongue, without the slightest effort or wish for fame or notoriety of any kind. In another sense, however, I do see that it has a meaning and interest for Englishmen in general, and have therefore consented to its publication in the usual way, though not without a sense of discomfort and annoyance at having the veil even partially lifted from the intimacies of a private family circle. For, in a noisy and confused time like ours, it does seem to me that most of us have need to be reminded of, and will be the better for bearing in mind, the reserve of strength and power which lies quietly at the nation's call, outside the whirl and din of public and fashionable life, and entirely ignored in the columns of the daily press. The subject of this memoir was only a good specimen of thousands of Englishmen of high culture, high courage, high principle, who are living their own quiet lives in every corner of the kingdom, from John o' Groat's to the Land's-End, bringing up their families in the love of God and their neighbour, and keeping the atmosphere around them clean, and pure and strong, by their example,—men who would come to the front, and might be relied on, in any serious national crisis.

One is too apt to fancy, from the photographs of the nation's life which one gets day by day, that the old ship has lost the ballast which has stood her in such good stead for a thousand years, and is rolling more and more helplessly, in a gale which shows no sign of abating, for her or any other national vessel, until at last she must roll over and founder. But it is not so. England is in less stress, and in better trim, than she has been in in many a stiffer gale.

The real fact is, that nations, and the families of which nations are composed, make no parade or fuss over that part of their affairs which is going right. National life depends on home life, and foreign critics are inclined to take the chronicles of our Divorce Court as a test by which to judge the standard of our home life, like the old gentleman who always spelt through the police reports to see " what the people were about." An acquaintance, however, with any average English neighbourhood, or any dozen English families taken at random, ought to be sufficient to reassure the faint-hearted, and to satisfy them that (to use the good old formula) the Lord has much work yet for this nation to do, and the nation manliness and godliness enough left to do it all, notwithstanding superficial appearances.

A life without sensation or incident may therefore well form a more useful subject of study in such a time, than the most exciting narrative of adventure and success, the conditions being, that it shall have been truly lived, and faithfully told. Readers will judge for themselves whether the former condition has been fulfilled in this case: I wish I could feel the same confidence as to the latter. I can only say I have done my best.

T. H.

Dedication.

TO MY NEPHEWS AND SONS.

My dear Boys,

It has pleased God to take to Himself the head of the family of which you are members. Most of you are too young to enter into the full meaning of those words "family" and "membership," but you all remember with sore hearts, and the deepest feeling of love and reverence, the gentle, strong, brave man, whom you used to call father or uncle; and who had that wonderful delight in, and attraction for, young folk, which most very gentle and brave men have. You are conscious, I know, that a great cold chasm has suddenly opened in your lives—that strength and help has gone away from you, to which you knew you might turn in any of the troubles which boys, and very young men, feel so keenly. Well, I am glad that you feel that it is so: I should not have much hope of you if it were otherwise. The chasm will close up, and you will learn, I trust and pray, where to go for strength and help, in this and all other troubles.

It is very little that I can do for you. Probably you can do more for me; and my need is even sorer than yours. But what I can do I will. Several of you have asked me questions about your father and uncle, what we used to do, and think and talk about, when he and I were boys together. Well, no one can answer these questions better than I, for we were as nearly of an age as brothers can be—I was only thirteen months younger—and we were companions from our childhood. We went together to our first school, when I was nearly eight and he nine years old; and then on to Rugby together; and were never separated for more than a week until he went to Oxford, where I followed a year later. For the first part of my time there, in college, we lived in the same rooms, always on the same staircase; and afterwards in the same lodgings. From that time to the day of his death we lived in the most constant intimacy and affection. Looking back over all those years, I can call to mind no single unkind, or unworthy, or untruthful, act or word of his; and amongst all the good influences for which I have to be thankful, I reckon the constant presence and example of his brave, generous, and manly life as one of the most powerful and ennobling. If I can in any measure reproduce it for you, I know that I shall be doing you a good service; and helping you, in even more difficult times than those in which we grew up, to quit yourselves as brave and true English boys and Englishmen, in whatever work or station God may be pleased to call you to.

You have all been taught to look to one life as your model, and to turn to Him who lived it on our earth, as to the guide, and friend, and helper, who alone can strengthen the feeble knees, and lift up the fainting heart. Just in so far as you cleave to that teaching, and follow that life, will you live your own faithfully. If I were not sure that what I am going to try to do for you would help to turn you more trustfully and lovingly to that source of all truth, all strength, all light, be sure I would not have undertaken it. As it is, I know it will be my fault if it does not do this.

THOMAS HUGHES.

CONTENTS.

CHAPTER I.
FIRST YEARS 1

CHAPTER II.
RUGBY 17

CHAPTER III.
A FATHER'S LETTERS 49

CHAPTER IV.
OXFORD 59

CHAPTER V.
DEGREE 80

CHAPTER VI.
START IN LIFE 88

CHAPTER VII.

1849–50: AN EPISODE 109

CHAPTER VIII.

ITALY 121

CHAPTER IX.

MIDDLE LIFE 130

CHAPTER X.

LETTERS TO HIS BOYS 151

CHAPTER XI.

CONCLUSION 170

MEMOIR OF A BROTHER.

CHAPTER I.

FIRST YEARS.

My brother was born on the 18th of September, 1821 at Uffington, in Berkshire, of which your great-grandfather was vicar. Uffington was then a very primitive village, far away from any high road, and seven miles from Wantage, the nearest town from which a coach ran to London. There were very few neighbours, the roads were almost impassable for carriages in the winter, and the living was a poor one; but your great-grandfather (who was a Canon of St. Paul's) had exchanged a much richer living for it, because his wife had been born there, and was deeply attached to the place. Three George Watts's had been vicars of Uffington, in direct succession from father to son, and she was the daughter of the last of them. So your grandfather, who was their only child, came to live in the village on his marriage, in an old farmhouse close to the church, to which your grandfather added some rooms, so as to make it habitable. If you should ever make a pilgrimage to the place, you will not find the house, for it has been pulled down; but the grand old church is there, and White Horse Hill, rising just behind the village, just as they were half a century ago, when we first looked at them. We could see the church from our bed-room window, and the hill from our nursery, a queer upper room amongst the rafters, at the top of the old part of the house, with a dark closet in one corner, into which the nurses used to put us when we were more unruly than usual. Here we lived till your great-grandfather's death, thirteen years later, when your grandfather removed to his house at Donnington.

The memories of our early childhood and boyhood throng upon me, so that I scarcely know where to begin, or what to leave out. I cannot, however, I am sure, go wrong in telling you, how I became first aware of a great difference between us, and of the effect the discovery had on me. In the spring of 1828, when he was seven and I six years old, our father and mother were away from home for a few days. We were playing together in the garden, when the footman came up to us, the old single-barrelled gun over his shoulder which the gardener had for driving away birds from the strawberries, and asked us whether we shouldn't like to go rook-shooting. We jumped at the offer, and trotted along by his side to the rookery, some 300 yards from the house. As we came up we saw a small group of our friends under the trees—the groom, the village schoolmaster, and a farmer or two—and started forwards to greet them. Just before we got to the trees, some of them began firing up at the young rooks. I remember, even now, the sudden sense of startled fear which came over me. My brother ran in at once under the trees, and was soon carrying about the powder-horn from one to another of the shooters. I tried to force myself to go up, but could not manage it. Presently he ran out to me, to get me to go back with him, but in vain. I could not overcome my first impression, and kept hovering round, at a distance of thirty or forty yards, until it was time for us to go back; ashamed of myself, and wondering in my small mind why it was that he could go in amongst that horrible flashing and smoke, and the din of firing, and cawing rooks, and falling birds, and I could not.

I had encountered the same puzzle in other ways already. Some time before my father had bought a small Shetland pony for us, Moggy by name, upon which we were to complete our own education in riding. We had already mastered the rudiments, under the care of our grandfather's coachman. He had been in our family thirty years, and we were as fond of him as if he had been a relation. He had taught us to sit up and hold the bridle, while he led a quiet old cob up and down with a leading rein. But, now that Moggy was come, we were to make quite a new step in horsemanship. Our parents had a theory that boys must teach themselves, and that a saddle (except for propriety, when we rode to a neighbour's house to carry a message, or had to appear otherwise in public) was a hindrance rather than a help. So, after our morning's lessons, the coachman used to take us to the paddock in which Moggy lived, put her bridle on, and leave us to our own devices. I could see that that moment was, from the first, one of keen enjoyment to my brother. He would scramble up on her back, while she went on grazing—without caring to bring her to the elm stool in the corner of the field, which was our mounting place—pull her head up, kick his heels into her sides, and go scampering away round the paddock with the keenest delight. He was Moggy's master from the first day, though she not unfrequently managed to get rid of him by sharp turns, or stopping dead short in her gallop. She knew it quite well; and, just as well, that she was mistress as soon as I was on her back. For weeks it never came to my turn without my wishing myself anywhere else. George would give me a lift up, and start her. She would trot a few yards, and then begin grazing, notwithstanding my timid expostulations, and gentle pullings at her bridle. Then he would run up, and pull up her head, and start her again, and she would bolt off with a flirt of her head, and never be content till

I was safely on the grass. The moment that was effected she took to grazing again, and I believe enjoyed the whole performance as much as George, and certainly far more than I did. We always brought her a carrot, or bit of sugar, in our pockets, and she was much more like a great good-tempered dog with us than a pony.

Our first hunting experience now came off. Some staghounds—the King's, if I remember rightly—came down for a day or two's sport in our part of Berkshire, and a deer was to be turned out on the downs, a few miles from our house. Accordingly the coachman was to take us both. I was to go before him on one of the carriage horses, made safe by a leather strap which encircled us both, while George rode Moggy. He was anxious to go unattached, but on the whole it was considered better that the coachman should hold a leading rein, as no one knew how Moggy might behave with the dogs, and no one but I knew how completely she would have to do as he chose. We arrived safely at the meet, saw the deer uncarted, the hounds laid on, and lumbered slowly after, till they swept away over a rise in the downs, and we saw them no more. So, after riding about for some time, the coachman produced some bread and cheese from his pocket, and we dismounted, and hitched up horse and pony on the leeward side of an old barn. We had not finished our lunch, when suddenly, to our intense delight, the stag cantered by within twenty yards of us, and, by the time we were on horseback again, the hunt followed. This time George and Moggy made the most desperate efforts for freedom, but the coachman managed to keep them in tow, and so the hunt went away from us again. I believe it was in consequence of George's remonstrances when he got home that it was now settled he should be allowed to go to the next meet of the foxhounds in our neighbourhood without a leading rein. This is his account of that great event, in a letter to his grandmother, almost the first he ever wrote. Those of you who have been brought up in the country will see how respectfully he always treats the fox, always giving him a capital F when he mentions him.

"UFFINGTON.

"DEAR GRANDMAMA,

"Your little dog Mustard sometimes teases the hawk by barking at him, and sometimes the hawk flies at Mustard. I have been out hunting upon our black pony, Moggy, and saw the Fox break cover, and the hounds follow after him. I rode fifteen miles. Papa brought me home the Fox's lug. I went up a great hill to see the hounds drive the Fox out of the wood. I saw Ashdown Park House: there is a fine brass nob at the top of it. Tom and I send best love to you and grandpapa.

"I am, your affectionate grandson,

"GEORGE HUGHES."

On this first occasion, as you may see by the letter, your grandfather was out with him, and he had not been allowed to follow. But soon afterwards his great triumph occurred, at a meet to which he and Moggy went off one morning after breakfast, in the wildest spirits. Your grandfather did not go out that day; so one of the farmers who happened to be going was to give an eye to Master George, and see that he got into no trouble, and found his way home. This he did about three o'clock in the afternoon, bearing the brush in his hand, with his face all covered with blood, after the barbarous custom of those days. He had been in at the death; and the honest farmer recounted to us in the broadest Berkshire the wonders which he and Moggy had performed together; creeping through impossible holes in great fences, scrambling along ditches and up banks to the finish, when he had been singled out from outside the ring of horsemen and led up to the master, the late Lord Ducie, to be "blooded" by the huntsman, and receive the brush, the highest honour the boy foxhunter can achieve.

And so it was with all our games and exercises, whether we were at football, wrestling, climbing, single-stick (which latter we were only allowed to practise in the presence of an old cavalry pensioner, who had served at Waterloo). He seemed to lay hold of whatever he put his hand to by the right end, and so the secret of it delivered itself up to him at once. One often meets with people who seem as if they had been born into the world with two left hands, and two left feet, and rarely with a few who have two right hands; and of these latter he was as striking an example as I have ever known. Often as a boy, and much oftener since, I have thought over this gift, trying to make out where the secret lay. For, though never very ambitious myself, I was more so than he was, and had the greatest wish to do every exercise and game as well as I possibly could; and by dint of real hard work, and years of practice, I did manage, in one or two instances, to reach the point which he had attained almost as it were by instinct. But I never could get nearer to his secret than this, that it lay in a sort of unconsciousness, which I believe to be natural courage. What I mean is, that what might possibly happen to himself never seemed to cross his mind: that he might get a fall and hurt himself, for instance, or get his head or his shins broken, or the like. And so, not being disturbed by any such considerations about himself, he had nothing to hinder him from just falling at once into the very best way of doing whatever he took in hand. Of course, even then, it required a fine body, as I have known boys and men, of equal natural courage, who were awkward and slow because they were very clumsily put together. But, on the other hand, I have known many men with equally fine bodies who never could get any decent work out of them. Now, with all the thinking in the world about it, I never could have acquired this natural gift; but, by having an example of it constantly before my eyes, I got the next best thing, which was a scorn of myself for feeling fear. This by degrees hardened into the habit of doing what I saw him do, and so I managed to pass through school and college without betraying the timidity of which I was ashamed.

Why do I make the confession now to you? Because I see the same differences in you that there were in us. One or two of you are naturally courageous, and the rest as naturally timid as I was. The first I hope will always bear with the others, and help them, as my brother helped me. If he had twitted me because I could not come under the trees at the rook-shooting, or because I was afraid of Moggy, I should probably never have felt the shame, or made the exertion, necessary to overcome my natural timidity. And to you who are not naturally courageous, I would say, make the effort to conquer your fear at once; you can't begin too early, and will never be worth much till you have made it.

But there was another natural difference between us which deserves a few words, as it will bring out his character more clearly to you; and that was, that he was remarkably quiet and reserved, and shy with strangers, and I the reverse. When we came down to dessert, after a dinner party, and had to stand by our father's side (as the custom was then in our parts), and say to each guest in turn, "Your good health, Sir, or Madam," while we sipped a little sweet wine and water, the ceremony was a torture to him; while to me it was quite indifferent, and I was only running my eye over the dishes, and thinking which I should choose when it came to my turn. In looking over his earliest letters, I find in one, written to his mother a few weeks after we first went to school, this passage: "We are both very well and happy. I find that I like Tom better at school than I do at home, and yet I do not know the reason." I was surprised for a moment when I came on this sentence. Of course, if love is genuine, the longer people know each other, the deeper it becomes; and therefore our friendship, like all others, grew richer and deeper as we got older. But this was the first time I ever had an idea that his feelings towards me changed after we went to school. I am not sure that I can give the reason any more than he could; but, on thinking it over, I daresay it had something to do with this difference I am speaking of.

I remember an old yeoman, a playfellow of our father's, who lived in a grey gabled house of his own at the end of the village in those days, and with whom we used to spend a good deal of our spare time, saying to a lady, about her sons, "Bring 'em up sarcy (saucy), Marm! I likes to see bwoys brought up sarcy." I have no doubt that he, and others, used to cultivate my natural gift of sauciness, and lead me on to give flippant answers, and talk nonsense. In fact, I can quite remember occasions of the kind, and George's quiet steady look at them, as he thought, no doubt, "What a fool my brother is making of himself, and what a shame of you to encourage him!" Apart altogether from his shyness, he had too much self-command and courtesy himself to run into any danger of this kind.

Now, the moment we got to school, my sauciness abated very rapidly on the one hand, and, on the other, I became much more consciously beholden to him. We had scarcely been there a week when the first crisis occurred which made us both aware of this fact. My form had a lesson in early Greek History to get up, in which a part of the information communicated was, that Cadmus was the first man who "carried letters from Asia to Greece." When we came to be examined, the master asked us, "What was Cadmus?" This way of putting it puzzled us all for a moment or two, when suddenly the words "carried letters" came into my head, and, remembering the man with the leather bag who used to bring my father's papers and letters, and our marbles and whipcord, from Farringdon, I shouted, "A postman, Sir." The master looked very angry for a moment, but, seeing my perfect good faith, and that I had jumped up expecting to go to the head of the form, he burst out laughing. Of course all the boys joined in, and when school was over I was christened Cadmus. That I probably should not have minded, but it soon shortened into "Cad," at which all the blood in my eight-year-old veins was on fire. The more angry I was, the more some of the boys persecuted me with the hateful name; especially one stupid big fellow of twelve or so, who ought to have been two forms higher, and revenged himself for his place amongst us little ones by making our small lives as miserable as he could. A day or two after, with two or three boys for audience, he had got me in a corner of the playground, into which he kept thrusting me violently back, calling me "Cad, Cad," while I was ready to fly at his throat and kill him. Suddenly we heard a step tearing down the gravel walk, and George, in his shirt sleeves, fresh from a game of rounders, rushed into the circle, and sent my tyrant staggering back with a blow in the chest, and then faced him with clenched fists, and a blaze in his eye, which I never saw there more than two or three times. I don't think many boys, or men, would have liked to face him when it was there. At any rate my persecutor didn't, though he must have been a stone heavier, and much stronger. So he slunk off, muttering to himself, to the disgust of the boys who hoped for a row, and I strutted out of my corner, while George went back to his rounders, after looking round and saying, "Just let me hear any of you call my brother 'Cad' again." I don't think I ever heard *that* nickname again at our first school, and it must have been very shortly after that he wrote home, "I find I like Tom better at school than I do at home, and yet I do not know the reason." The strongest and most generous natures are always fondest of those who lean on them.

But I am getting on faster than I intended. We have not quite got away from home yet. And now let me turn again to my story. You will, I am sure, be interested by the following letter, which was written to us by Miss Edgeworth. You probably have never read her books; but in our day, when there were very few children's books, they were our great delight, and almost the only ones we possessed, after "Robinson Crusoe," "The Pilgrim's Progress," and "Sandford and Merton." I forget how we discovered that the lady who wrote "Frank and Rosamond" was really alive, and that our grandmother actually had met her, and knew her. But, having made the discovery, we laid our heads together, and wrote two letters, asking her to tell us what were the contents of the remaining drawers in the wonderful Indian cabinet. Our grandmother sent her the letters, and in due time we received the following reply:—

"EDGEWORTH'S TOWN, *July* 20*th*, 1828.

"To my dear young readers, GEORGE and THOMAS HUGHES.

"I am glad that you can write as well as read; your two letters were both very well written, and I had pleasure in reading them. I am glad that you like Harry and Lucy and Frank and Rosamond. I wish I could tell you anything more that would entertain you about the other nine drawers of the India cabinet; but what I am going to tell you will disappoint you I daresay, and I cannot help it. When Rosamond opened the 4th drawer she found in it—nothing—but a sheet of white paper at the bottom of the drawer, and on the paper was written only the word *China*. The writing was in a large round hand, like that in which your letter to me was written. Rosamond shut this drawer and opened the next, which was the 5th—empty! On the paper at the bottom of this drawer, in the same handwriting, was *Constantinople*. The 6th, the 7th, the 8th which she opened, one after another as fast as she could, were all empty! On the paper in the 6th drawer, which was very deep, was written—*The North Pole and Iceland—Norway—Sweden and Lapland.* In the 8th drawer was written *Rome and Naples—Mount Vesuvius and Pompeii.* At the bottom of the 9th drawer, *Persia—Arabia and India.*

"Then on the paper in the 9th drawer was written in small-hand and cramped writing without lines, and as crookedly as might be expected from a first attempt without lines, what follows:—

"'I, little Matt. (which is short for Matthew), promise my dear good kindest of all aunts, Aunt Egerton, whom I love best in the world, that when I am grown up *quite* to be a great man, and when I go upon my travels as I intend to do when I am old enough and have money enough, I will bring her home all the greatest curiosities I can find for her in every country for these drawers. I have written in them the names of the countries I intend to visit, therefore I beg my dear aunt will never put anything in these 9 drawers till my curiosities come home. I will unpack them myself. N.B.—I have begun this morning to make a list from my book of travels and voyages of all the curiosities I think worthy my bringing home for the India cabinet.' (M. E.—A true copy.)

"My dear young readers, this is all I know about the matter. I am sorry I can tell you no more; but to no one else have I ever told so much. This letter is all for yourselves—from one who would like to see you very much, and who hopes that you would like her too if you knew

her, though you might not like her at first sight; for she is neither young nor pretty, but an old good-natured friend,
  (Signed)   "Maria Edgeworth."

In the winter, before we went to school first, we were left alone at home, for the first time, while our parents paid some visits. George was left in charge of the house (under the governess), with injunctions to see that all things went on regularly in the village. Our mother's Saturday clothing club was to be held as usual, and we were not to neglect either the poor, or the birds, who were fed daily through the winter on a table on the lawn, just outside the dining-room window. The following letter will show you how conscientiously the trust was fulfilled :—

"Dear Mama,   "*January* 21*st*, 1830.

"We are all well, and quite free from colds. All the people brought their money correctly last Saturday. Tims had his chimney began more than a week ago, and no doubt it is finished by this time. I have told cook about making broth and gruel for any who are sick. We constantly feed all your birds, and they eat as much as would give baby two meals. We shall be glad to see you and Papa.

"I am, your dutiful son,
      "George Hughes."

One other letter I will give to amuse you. You elder boys will say, that if he hadn't learnt to answer questions better when he went to school, he would never have taken a high degree at Oxford :—

"My dear Mama, "*January 26th*, 1830.

"We thank you for the conundrums you sent us, and I think we have found out two of them :—'If all the letters were asked out to dinner, which of them would not go?' The one that asked them would not go. 'What thing is that which lights the eyes, yet never fails to blind?' The sun. You must tell us when you write whether these are right or not. We cannot find out the other one. Give my love to papa, and tell him that I will write to him next week. We shall be delighted to see you home again. I think I am going on well with my Latin, and I hope Papa will be satisfied with me.

"I am, your affectionate son,
"George Hughes."

We went to school together, in the autumn of this year, at Twyford, near Winchester. On the way there we stayed a few days at Lyndhurst, in the New Forest, at the house of an old naval officer. He had another house near us in Berkshire, our favourite resort, as there were several little girls in the family of our own age, all very pretty. One of these little ladies took a fancy to some water-flower, as we were walking in the forest, the day before the school met. Without saying a word, George just jumped into the pond, and fetched it for her; thereby ruining a new suit of clothes (as your grandmother remarked) and risking his life, for there was no one but a nurse with us, and it was just as likely that the pond might be out of his depth as not. However, as it happened, no harm came of it, and we went on next day to Twyford.

CHAPTER II.

RUGBY.

WE stayed at Twyford till the end of 1833, when our father resolved to send us to Rugby. Dr. Arnold had been a little his junior at Oriel; and, though considerably exercised by the Doctor's politics, he shared that unhesitating faith in his character and ability which seems to have inspired all his contemporaries. In the meantime George had gone up rapidly into the highest form at Twyford, amongst boys two years older than himself, and generally carried off not only prizes for the school work but for all kinds of gymnastics. Twyford was a little before its time in this respect, as we had quite a number of gymnastic poles of different kinds in the playground, upon which we had regular lessons under a master who came over from Winchester. Every half-year we had a gymnastic examination, attended by the master's daughters, and a lady or two from the neighbourhood, who distributed the prizes (plates of fruit and cake) at the end of the day to the successful boys. One special occasion I well remember, in which the excitement ran particularly high. A new prize for vaulting was to be given, not for the common style "which any boy could do," our master said; but for vaulting between the hands. I don't want any of you to try it, for it is a dangerous exercise, and I wonder that some of us did not break our necks in attempting it. You had to place both your hands on the back of the vaulting horse, as far apart, or as near together, as you liked, and then spring over between them without lifting either, even for half an inch. Of course none but long-armed boys could do it at all; but there were enough of these for a large entry. Very soon, however, one after another fell out, either for touching with their feet, or shifting a hand during the vault; and George and a very active boy, a great friend of ours in after years, Charles Mansfield by name, were left alone. They two went on springing over the horse, without the least touch of foot or shifting of hand, until it was at last voted by acclamation that they should divide the great plate of grapes, apples, and sponge cakes, which stood ready for the winner.

But I must not tell you so much of all his successes in athletic games. These things are made too much of nowadays, until the training and competitions for them outrun all rational bounds. What I want to show you is, that while he was far more distinguished in these than any of you are at all likely to be (or indeed, as things stand, than I for one should wish you to be), he never neglected the real purpose of a schoolboy's life for them, as you will see from some of his early letters from Rugby, to which school we went in February 1834, when he was only twelve years old. These are all addressed to his father and mother, and generally end, "Please consider this for grandmama as well as for yourselves." No boy was ever more thoughtful of every one who had any possible claim upon him. Here is almost the first of them.

"Rugby, *April 25th*, 1834.

"My dear Papa and Mama,

"I received your letter to-day. I have got a little cough now, but it is getting better every day. Tom is quite well. I now generally keep among the four first of my form, and I find that by application you are enabled to do yourself greater credit than if you trust yourself to the assistance of books or that of other boys. There are two boys besides myself who always do our work together, and we always take three-quarters of an hour out of school, besides three-quarters which is allowed us in school, to prepare our work. The work of our form is the Eumenides of Æschylus, Homer, Virgil, Horace, and Cicero's Epistles. The half year is divided into two quarters, one of which is for classics mostly, and the other for history. The books for the next quarter are Arrian's Expedition of Alexander, and Paterculus's History of Rome, and Mackintosh's English History. For Composition we do Greek Iambics and Latin Verse, which is generally taken from some English author, and we translate it into Latin. We also do English and Latin themes once a week. The Easter business is just over; there were three speech days, the rehearsal (or first day), the day on which the poor people are allowed to come, and the grand day. On the grand day the day was very fine, and there was a very large assembly of people. The speeches and prize compositions and poems were—

Sixth Form.

Lake.[1]—Latin essay: Bellum civile Mariannum.
Lake.—Latin verse: Phœnicia.
Clough.[2]—English essay: The English language.
Clough.—English verse: Close of eighteenth century.
Arnold.[3]—Greek verse: The murder of Becket.

Fifth Form Essay.

Jacson.—On the Sources of Pleasure.
Emeris.—Speech of Canning at Lisbon.
Simpkin.—Conclusion of Warren Hastings' trial.

"The speeches began at one o'clock; they were ended at three, and about 200 went to dine at the 'Spread Eagle.' Here Dr. Arnold gained a complete triumph over Litchfield and Boughton Leigh, who wanted to prevent his health being drunk on account of his politics, or their private malice. I have not much more to say now. Give my love to cousins, uncle, grandmama, and everybody.

"I remain, your affectionate Son,

"G. E. Hughes."

He writes home of everything, in these first years, except of what he knew would only give pain, and be quite

---

[1] Now Dean of Durham.   [2] A. H. Clough, the poet.
[3] The Rev. C. Arnold, of Rugby.

useless—the exceedingly rough side of school life as it then existed. A small boy might be, and very frequently was, fagged for every moment of his play hours day after day; and there was a good deal of a bad kind of bullying. But these things he took as a matter of course, making the best of what was inevitable. He used often afterwards to declare, that the boys of that generation made the best fields at cricket he had ever seen, and to set it down to the unmerciful amount of fagging they had to go through. Escape out of bounds before you were caught by a sixth form boy, was the only remedy; and, once out of bounds, there was the river for amusement, and the railway, upon which large gangs of navigators had just been put to work. George became a skilful fisherman, and a most interested watcher of the earthworks, and duly chronicles how he has caught a big eel in one letter; in another, how "the railway is going on very fast: they have nearly filled up one valley, and carried it over a stream;" in a third how "Mr. Wombwell's show of wild beasts has come in, I believe the finest in England," and including "four elephants, a black tiger and tigress, and two lions, one of which was the famous Wallace who fought the dogs."

Before the end of the second year he had got through three forms, and was nearly the head of the fags, and anxious to try his hand for the single scholarship, which was then offered at Rugby for boys under fourteen. As there was only one, of course the competition was a very severe one. But his first letter of that year contains a passage too characteristic to pass over. So I must leave the scholarship for a moment. We, with other boys who lived in Berkshire and Hampshire, were often obliged to post, or hire a coach to ourselves, as there was only one regular coach a day on those cross-country roads. We used to make up parties accordingly, and appoint one boy to manage the whole business, who had rather a hard time of it, while all the rest enjoyed themselves in the most uproarious manner. George was soon selected as the victim, and bearer of the common purse; and his conscientious struggles with post-boys and hostlers, landlords and waiters, cost him, I am sure, more pain and anxiety than all the scholarship examinations he ever went in for. Thus he writes in February 1836, to tell of our safe arrival, and then goes on:—

"We had just enough money to pay our journey. The worst of it is, that every postboy, when they see that they are driving boys, at the end of the stage, when you pay them their money, are never contented, and say, 'never given less than so and so;' and, 'shall be kept up all night;' 'roads bad,' &c. &c., and keep on bothering you till you really don't know what to do. However, that is over now, and we are fairly settled again at Rugby, and very comfortable."

And then, at the end of the half, when he has to begin arranging for the return journey, "the Doctor will not take any account of these plaguey postboys, and so always allows us too little journey money."

"*December* 11*th*, 1836.—About our journey money ;. I do not think that Dr. Arnold gives us quite enough. I suppose he does not exactly know the distance we have to go. He only gives us 30*s*. each. I think you always give us 6*l*. (or 2*l*. apiece) to go there, which just takes us, including everything."

We were always encouraged to bring our friends home, but how scrupulous he was about using the privilege the remainder of the letter just quoted will show you :—

"There is a boy who will go all the way home with us— G——. He is a præpostor. He is going as far as Newbury that day, where he is going to sleep, and go on in the Oxford coach to Winchester, where he stops. Would you think it any inconvenience to give him a bed? It is not, however, of the least consequence, only I think that being a stranger in those parts he would take it kindly, and be able to return the favour to Walter or Tom at Rugby. If you think it the least inconvenience pray tell me, for it does not signify one jot: I have not said a word to him on the subject yet. We begin to smell the approach of the holidays; the bills are being made up, the trunks brought down, the clothes cleaned, &c. &c. I shall take care to peep into the Museum on my road through Oxford, as I did not half satisfy my curiosity before. I am glad to hear that Dumple goes well in harness; also that the wild ducks "habitant in flumine nostro, quos ego, maxime gaudeo;" that Mr. Majendie has approved of my Lyric verses, which, however, I cannot think merit such commendation. There has been a great balloon mania in the school lately; everybody has been making a balloon. We set them off with spirits of wine lighted under them, and then run after them. They generally go about five miles, and we always recover them after a hard run. I have cut one out myself from tissue paper, and I will bring it home that I may have the pleasure of setting it off before Jenny. I think she would like to see it."

But I am forgetting the scholarship.

"Rugby, *March* 16, 1836.

"I will now tell you what I was examined in for the scholarship; 1st, in composition, Latin theme; subject, 'Est natura hominum novitatis avida,' which, as you may imagine, was very easy; Latin verse, 'The Battle of Thermopylæ;' English theme, 'Painting,' also very easy. In the Latin verse I did seventeen verses in two hours, which was more than any other of the candidates, and I quite satisfied myself in the other two subjects. In Latin construing we had a passage from Virgil and Cæsar, and in Greek, Homer's Odyssey. We were also examined in St. Paul, and, thanks to your abbreviation, I answered all the questions. We have yet to be examined in Mackintosh, French, and mathematics.

"I think now I have satisfied you with respect to the work of the scholarship."

In his next of April 2nd, he communicates the result as follows, but not mentioning that six of his competitors were older than he, and in higher forms :—

"We are all quite well. I did not get the scholarship, but I was third. I have been promoted out of the lower into the middle fifth, and I am doing very well in it. We read Demosthenes, Thucydides, Cicero in Verrem, and the Antigone of Sophocles. The great examination at the end of the half is soon going to be set. The middle fifth and upper fifth are examined together, and if I do well in it I may be high up in the fifth at the end of the half."

He did well, as usual, and got into the fifth at the summer examination. Your grandmother had a small bookcase made on purpose for our prizes, which was being rapidly filled by George. He writes thus to her just before our holidays :—

"*June 6th*, 1836.—I have got some good news for you. I have got an addition to your rosewood bookcase, *alias* a prize. It's called 'Rickman's Architecture.' It is very nicely bound, and has some nice pictures of abbeys and churches, with a description of all the fine cathedrals and large churches, amongst which I saw our old Uffington church. Donnington Castle was also mentioned."

On returning as a fifth form boy he describes the fifth form room, of which he is now free, with great delight, and reverence for its "two sofas, three tables, curtains, and large bookcase," and adds—

"I have got a nice double study to myself, but I wish I had some more books, since I think that nothing makes a study look so nice as books. I must bring some to Rugby next half; I can take care of them now. I have lately been engaged in making an English verse translation of a chorus in the Eumenides, and I will give it you, if you think it worth while reading. I wish you would criticize it as much as you can. I know it is very imperfect, but as it is the first regular copy of English verse I ever did, I think it is pretty good for me. Here it is," &c.

But I shall not copy it out for fear of tiring you, and indeed I feel that I must hurry over the rest of his school life. When every line and word is full of life and interest to oneself, it is perhaps hard to judge where to stop for the next generation. A few short extracts, however, from his letters during his last three years will, I think, interest you. At least some of the references will show you what a time of revolution you were born into. When we were your ages there was no railway between London and Birmingham: and in all other directions, and on all other sides of English life, the change seems to me quite as great as in this of locomotion.

"*April* 1837.—They are getting on very fast with the railroad, and I hear that it is to be finished in August. I intend going to-morrow to Kilsby to see a very large tunnel that they are making for the railroad there.

"There has been a row about fishing. Mr. Boughton Leigh's keeper took away a rod from a fellow who was fishing in a part of the river that has always been given to the fellows to fish in, but which the keeper said was a preserve of Mr. Leigh's. The fellows went in a body to Mr. Leigh's house, but found he had gone to London; they are going to write a letter to him, asking the reason of taking the rod. The fellow who had his rod taken away has caught an immense quantity of pike, and this half he caught in one afternoon two, one 5 lbs., the other three."

"*June* 1837.—I dare say you will be glad to hear that Stanley [1] has got the English verse; they say it is the best since Heber's Palestine that has been written; some part of it was quoted in the 'Standard.' Vaughan [2] also has got the Porson's Greek verse, and the Greek Ode and Epigrams."

"*September* 1837.—There was a meeting at Rugby a little while ago, got up by some horrid Radicals, about paying Church rates, whether they should pay them or not; but there was a very large majority that they should pay them; although half the town are Dissenters, and another quarter Radicals."

"*November.*—I suppose Tom has told you that I have been raised to the sixth form, and am now a præpostor. I do not find the work much harder than it was in the fifth. A Mr. Walker, philosophical lecturer, has just been here, and when he found the fellows would not come to his lectures, and heard that they were playing football, delivered himself of this elegant sentence, 'Brutes, to prefer football to philosophy!' which you may imagine caused a laugh, and did not at all further his object of procuring an audience. This same person afterwards caused an article to be put into the *Northampton Herald* complaining of the conduct of Dr. Arnold, in not allowing the boys to go without permission of their parents. Yesterday the school house, after a resistance of six days, were beaten; but it is not quite certain about whether it was a goal or not, and perhaps we shall play it again. The classing examination is just going

---

[1] Now Dean of Westminster.   [2] Master of the Temple.

to begin. I believe I am pretty well prepared. Clough has gone. Dr. Arnold has been away at London, at an examination of London University. Dr. Arnold's two sons are now at Rugby, having left Winchester. I have changed my study, and have now a horribly dark place in the bottom passage, which it is the fate of the bottom præpostor in the house to have, but I shall leave it next half."

"*March* 1838.—I write to tell you that I should like to write for one of the prizes, as I think it will be a good exercise for me; I have no particular choice, but I should prefer either the English prose, 'On the increased facility of local communication, and its probable effects on society,' or the Latin verse 'On the abdication of Charles the Fifth;' and I wish you would tell me which you think the best.

"The London and Birmingham Railroad has been opened from Rugby to Birmingham, and also from Stoney Stratford to London, but, in consequence of Kilsby tunnel falling in, it will not yet be opened the whole way: it is opened all the way now except thirty miles in the middle. I saw one of the trains go by yesterday for the first time in my life, and I was very much astonished."

"*June* 1838.—Have you read Mr. Dickens' 'Nicholas Nickleby?' I liked it very much, though I thought some parts of it are very much exaggerated and unnatural; particularly that about the school, if you have read it. I am sure no one could help laughing at it; but I think 'Oliver Twist' much superior.

"The Great London and Birmingham Railroad is to be opened throughout to-morrow week, I believe, so there will be no more coaches to bother us."

About this time a scribbling fever attacked the upper boys at Rugby. A year or two earlier the *Rugby Magazine* had gained considerable repute, from the publication of some of Clough's early poems, and contributions by others of the Stanley and Vaughan generation; and had thus furnished a healthy local outlet for the literary secretions of the sixth form. But that journal was now no more, so we were thrown back on the periodicals of the outside world. To get a copy of verses, or a short article, into one of these, was looked upon as an heroic feat, like making fifty runs in a school match. And of all the magazines, and they were much fewer in those days, Bentley's was the favourite; chiefly, I think, because of the "Ingoldsby Legends," which were then coming out in it. Mr. Barham was an old friend of your grandfather; and I believe it was through him that George had the pleasure of seeing himself in print for the first time. The editor accepted some translations of Anacreon, which he had done out of school-hours. Here are two specimens, and though I do not care to see any of you writing for magazines, I should be glad to think that you could render a classic so well at the age of seventeen:—

ANACREON MADE EASY.

η γη μελαινα πινει.

The dark earth drinks the heaven's refreshing rain;
   Trees drink the dew; the ocean drinks the air;

The sun the ocean drinks; the moon again
    Drinks her soft radiance from the sun's bright glare.
Since all things drink, then—earth, and trees, and sea,
    And sun and moon are all on quaffing set,
Why should you quarrel, my good friends, with me,
    Because I love a pot of heavy wet?

Θελω λεγειν Ατρειδας

I wished the two Atreidæs' fame to sing,
    And woke my lyre to a bold martial strain,
In vain, alas! for when I touched the string,
    The song to love and Cupid turned again.
I changed my string, then my whole lyre, I vow
    Nought *would* come out but sentiment and sighs,
Till Cupid broke my numskull with his bow:
    "Learn your own place, presumptuous, and be wise.
If you sport epic verses, for your pains
    Nought will you get, of that one fact I'm cartin.
Leave to old Grinding Homer blood and brains,
    And stick to *me*, old boy, I'll make your fortin."

When "Bentley" arrived at the school-house we were all in astonishment, and not a little uplifted at this feat, which seemed to link the school-house to the great world of literature. George took it very quietly, mentioning it thus in his next letter home:—

"*Sept.* 1838.—' 'Tis pleasant, sure, to see oneself in print. I saw my production in Mr. Bentley's last number by the side of much more deserving ones: I was very much amused with the last number, particularly with the report of the proceedings of the Mudfog Association. The idea of giving the young noblemen and gentlemen a place on purpose for their pranks was delightful, and likely I should think to knock that sort of thing on the head."

We now went always by rail to London, the guards of those days allowing us, for some time, to travel outside, where we scrambled about amongst the luggage, and climbed down into the carriages while the train was going. I often wonder that none of us broke our necks, especially the present Scotch Secretary of the Treasury, W. Adam, who was the most reckless of us all at these exploits. We always managed, during our few hours in town, to call on some of our father's literary friends, who were wonderfully kind to us. Here is a specimen :—

"*March* 1839.—I then went and called on Mr. Barham, and we went for a walk, first up into St. Paul's Library, where I saw some very fine books. We then went to Drury Lane Theatre, and Mr. Barham got us tickets for that night from Mr. Peake, who is, I believe, stage manager. It was curious to see the difference between the theatre in the daytime, and when it was lighted up at night. We then went to the Garrick Club and saw all the pictures there, which were very interesting. We went to Drury Lane that night and saw Mr. Van Amburgh and his lions, which was the only thing worth seeing in the evening. I saw some other lions, authors, &c. whom Mr. Barham knew; I am sure I think he knows everybody. I must not forget to tell you that we went through Alsatia, to a coal wharf Mr. Barham wanted to visit.

"Have you seen Sir Robert Peel's speech about the

Corn Laws? I should think he must have tired his legs and his lungs both, before he sat down: I don't understand much about it, but it seems to cause a good deal of excitement."

In the summer of 1839 he went in for the Exhibition examination, and did so well that his success in 1840 (his last year) was almost a certainty. But he did not remain for another examination, and I must tell you the reason of his leaving before his time, because, though I was then furiously on the other side, I think now that he was in the wrong. It was one of those curious difficulties which will happen, I suppose, every now and then in our great public schools, where the upper boys have so much power and responsibility, and in which there are (or were) a number of customs and traditions as to discipline, which are almost sacred to the boys, but scarcely recognized by the masters.

It happened thus. Just at this time the sixth form boys were on the average smaller and younger than usual, while there were a great number of big boys, not high up in the school, but excellent cricketers and football players, and otherwise manly and popular fellows. They swarmed in the eleven, and big-side football, and were naturally thrown very much with George and his friend Mackie.[1] In some houses, no doubt, they were inclined

---

[1] Afterwards M.P. for Dumfriesshire, a fine scholar and great athlete, who died only nine months before his old friend.

rather to ignore the authority of the sixth themselves, and of course their example was followed by the fags, so that the discipline of the school began to fall out of gear. At last matters came to a crisis. Some of the sixth form took to reporting to the Doctor cases which, according to school traditions, they ought to have dealt with themselves; and in other ways began to draw the reins too tightly. There were "levies" (as we called them) of the sixth and fifth, at which high words passed, and several of the sixth were sent to Coventry. This made the Doctor very angry, and he took the side of the disciplinarians. Then came a rebellious exhibition of fireworks one evening in the quadrangle. Then an Italian, with a lot of plaster casts, committed the unpardonable sin of coming into the Close without leave, and his wares were taken, and put up for "cock-shyes." He went straight to the Doctor, who insisted that the sixth should discover and report the offenders; but those who would could not, and those who might would not. The Doctor's face had been getting blacker and blacker for some time, and at last, one November morning, he sent half a dozen of the big fifth and middle fifth boys home, and told George and his friend Mackie, and one or two other sixth form boys, that they could not return after the end of the half-year.

And here I will give you two of your grandfather's letters to us on these matters, to show you how we were brought up. He was an old Westminster himself, and so quite understood the boys' side of the dispute.

He begins to George, telling him first about home doings, and then goes on :—

"I have received a letter from Dr. Arnold deserving attention, by which it appears that you have been remiss in your duties as a præposter, though he speaks fairly enough as to your own personal conduct. He alludes particularly to the letting off of fireworks, and the man whose images were broken, in neither of which you appear to have shown due diligence in discovering or reporting the boys concerned. Moreover, he thinks that those præposters who have been more active in enforcing the school routine have been unjustly treated with contempt and insult by the larger party of the boys—in fact, either bullied, or cut; and evidently he thinks that you have been amongst the cutters. Now, it is impossible for me to enter into the exact merits of the case at a distance; and possibly I may not be inclined to see it in all its details with the eye of a zealous schoolmaster; but, as you are now of a thinking age, I will treat the matter candidly to you, as a man of the world and a man of business, in which capacities I hope to see you efficient and respected in the course of a few years. Your own conduct seems to be gentlemanly and correct. Very good; this is satisfactory as far as it goes. But clearly, by the regulations of the school, you have certain duties to perform, the strict execution of which may in some cases be annoying to your own feelings, and to that *esprit de corps* which always exists among boys. Nevertheless, they must be performed. Those young men who have a real regard for the character of their school, which all of you are ready enough to stickle for when you get outside its walls, must not allow it to become a mere blackguard bear-garden, and to stink in the nostrils of other public schools, by tolerating, in those they are expected to govern, such things as they would not do themselves. When you grow a little older you will soon perceive that there is no situation in life worth having, and implying any respect, where moral firmness is not continually required, and unpleasant duties are to be performed. Were you now in the army, you would find that if you were not strict enough with your men, you would have a pack of drunkards and pilferers under your command, disgracing the regiment; and would receive a hint from your Colonel, in double quick time, to mend your vigilance or sell out. Ditto, if you were older and a college tutor. I remember a clever, amiable, and learned man, whom our young fellows used to laugh at behind his back, and play tricks on before his face, because he laboured under such a nervous gentlemanly scrupulousness that he could not say Bo to a goose, and therefore they learned little under him. I find myself that a magistrate has many harsh and disagreeable duties to perform, but he must perform them, or the law of the land becomes an old song, and his own person ridiculous. So that, in fact, I only urge you to conform yourself, like a sensible person, to the general condition of human life. I am inclined to think that the slackness in your case has arisen more from constitutional ease of temper than for fear of what a clique of disorderly fellows might say of you: for if it had been the latter motive, I am sure you had it not by inheritance from your mother or me. But this ease of temper may be carried to a fault. In a word, you must correct it forthwith in your conduct as a præposter, if you expect that I can treat you, as I wish to do, in the light of a young man, and a responsible person: as to my affection, you will always have that, so long as your own conduct is good. Now as to those crackers; you must have known the thing was childish and dangerous, and forbidden for good reasons. Remember poor Harrow.[1] Therefore you might have interposed in a firm and civil way, and prevented it on pain of instant report to the master, and no one could have complained that you did anything ungentlemanly. As to the fellows who broke the poor man's images and would not fork out the damage, I wish you had been more successful, perhaps more active, in discovering them; if you had broken their heads I could not have blamed you. But on this I must write to Tom. So good bye; and if you really value my respect for your character, look sharper to your police department. Remember you are no longer a child."

Then, on the same sheet, follows a letter to me. I must explain that I had been one of the image breakers, but had come forward with one of the others and paid the damage.

"I have heard an account of the affair of the images. You should have remembered, as a Christian, that to insult the poor is to despise the ordinance of God in making them so: and moreover, being well born and well bred, and having lived in good company at home, which, may be, has not been the privilege of all your schoolfellows, you should feel that it is the hereditary pride and duty of a gentleman to protect those who perhaps never sat down to a good meal in their lives. It would have been more manly and creditable if you had broken the head of ——, or some

---

[1] There had recently been a fireworks row at Harrow, the details of which had got into the newspapers, creating much scandal.

pompous country booby in your back settlement, than smashed the fooleries of this poor Pagan Jew, which were to him both funds and landed estate. This strict truth obliges me to say, though, if you had bought his whole stock to indulge the school with a cock-shy, I should only have said 'A fool and his money are soon parted.' It is impossible, however, to be angry with you, as you came forward like a lad of spirit and gentlemanly feeling to repair your share, and perhaps more than your share, of the damage. The anxiety the poor fellow had suffered you could not make up to him. And it is well that you did make such reparation as you did; had it not been the case, you never would have recovered the place you would have lost in my esteem. Remember, this sort of thing must never happen again if you value that esteem. And have no acquaintance you can avoid with the stingy cowards who shirked their share of the damage: they can be no fit company for you or any gentleman. I don't know what the public opinion of Rugby says of them. We plain spoken old Westminsters, in the palmy days of the school, should have called them dirty dogs; and so much for them, more words than they are worth. I am glad to find that your general conduct is approved by the Doctor: and now that you have put your hand to the plough, don't take it off; and God bless you."

In conclusion, *to George:*—

"Don't cut, or look shy on, any of the præposters who have done their duty, if you do not think they are acting from private pique, or love of power. This question you have sense and honesty to decide for yourself. I have hinted to Arnold that it *may* be so, but cannot know it as well as you do, yea or nay. And if you do your own duty without flinching, your opinion will have weight with all whom it may concern. The Doctor evidently thinks you could be of essential use to him if you liked, and I am sure he is much too fair and honourable a man to want to make spies of his pupils. If you do not back him in what he has a right to enforce, you pass a tacit censure on a man you profess to esteem."

George's answer produced the following from your grandfather:—

"I like the tone of your vindication much. It shows the proper spirit which I wish to cultivate, and a correct sense of what your duties are as a member of society. Be assured that I hate as much as you do the character of a talebearer and meddler, and a fellow who takes advantage of a little brief authority to gratify his own spite and love of importance. And in my reply to Dr. Arnold I said, that having been bred up on the system of 'study to be quiet and mind your own business,' you might very likely have fallen into the extreme of non-interference; which I thought was the best extreme for a gentleman to follow. I also hinted that his pets might not be quite immaculate in their motives, or deserve the good opinion of the more gentlemanly boys of their own standing, who had a right to form their own judgment and limit their own acquaintance, though not to interfere with the discipline of the school. What you have said of the fellow who caused the expulsion (rustication I should call it) of the others, confirms me. His conduct, in fact, if his words could be proved, deserves a round robin to Arnold from the school; and if you are sure it is so, I will back you with my full sanction in cutting any such malicious rascal. I think you will see after this that I do not speak from the notions of a pedant or a disciplinarian, and that I do not care two straws how you stand in the opinion of Doctor this, or Doctor that, provided you deserve your own good opinion as a Christian and a gentleman, and do justice to good principles and good blood, for which things you are indebted to sources independent of Rugby. But with all this I do not abandon my position, of which indeed you seem convinced, that order must be enforced at the expense of disagreeable duties. All I wish is this: put Dr. A. out of the question if you please, and enter into the views of the parents of the junior boys as if they were your own family friends: with this view you will not only protect their sons in their little comforts and privileges, but steadily check those habits in them which might render them nuisances in general society, or involve them in scrapes at school. After all, Arnold was right as to the prevention of crackers in the quadrangle, and you ought to have stopped it; on this point you say nothing. As to the investigation of the image matter: if you were not there at the time, you may not be blameable for want of success, and if they expected you to pump Tom, or employ any underhand means in getting at the truth, they knew but little of your family habits. Albeit, I wish the thing could have been traced. It was mean and cowardly, and, if it happened often, ruinous to the character of the school, inasmuch as the fellows did not step forward at once in a manly way and say, 'We were certainly wrong, and ready to pay for the cock-shy; but the parrots and Napoleons were irresistible.' The Doctor would have laughed, and approved. I do not wonder he was sore on the subject, feeling like a gentleman for the character of his school, as Lord B—— would have done for the character of his own parish, had a stranger had his pocket picked in it. Nor do I want you to adopt all his views or partialities. Only suppose yourself in his place: fancy what you would have a right to expect, and

remember that it cannot be done without the help of the
præposters. This you seem inclined to do, and you may
do it on your own independent footing, looking as coldly
as you please on any clique whose motives may be different
from your own. You have no need to court anybody's
favour if you cultivate the means of making yourself independent; and if you only fear God in the true sense, you
may snap your fingers at everything else,—which ends all
I have to say on this point. 'Upright and downright' is
the true motto."

I believe that no boy was ever more regretted. Since
he had been in the sixth, and especially in his last year,
when he was the Captain of Big-side Football and third
in the Eleven, bullying had disappeared from the school-
house, and house fagging had lost its irksomeness. The
House had regained its position, having beaten the
School at football. He had kicked the last goal from
"a place" nearly sixty yards from the post. The tradition
of that kick was handed down for many years, and, I
remarked, was always getting back some few yards; so
that, by the time it expired, I have no doubt it had
reached 100 yards, and become as fabulous as many
other traditions. His rule was perhaps rather too easy.
The loafers, who are always too numerous, had a much
better time than they deserved; and I doubt whether
the school-house first lessons were done so well as at
other times; for, instead of each boy going off to his
own study after supper, and stern silence reigning in the

passages till bed-time, groups of bigger boys would collect round the fires, and three or four fags in one study; and thus much time which should have been given to themes and verses was spent in talking over football and cricket matches, and the Barby and Crick runs at hare and hounds. I know that George himself regretted very much what had occurred, and I believe, had he had a second chance, would have dealt vigorously with the big boys at once. But he had to learn by the loss of his exhibition, as you will all have to learn in one way or another, that neither boys nor men *do* get second chances in this world. We all get new chances till the end of our lives, but not second chances in the same set of circumstances; and the great difference between one boy and another is, how he takes hold of, and uses, his first chance, and how he takes his fall if it is scored against him.

At the end of the half, Dr. Arnold, with his usual kindness, and with a view I believe to mark his approval of my brother's character and general conduct at the school, invited him to spend part of his holidays at the Lakes. His visit to Foxhow, and Yorkshire, at Christmas 1839, before he went up to Oxford, delighted him greatly. He had never seen a mountain before, and the fact of seeing them for the first time from his old master's house, with schoolfellows to whom he was warmly attached, doubled his pleasure. I have only room, however, for one of his letters:—

"Foxhow, *Jan. 6th,* 1840.

"My dear Father and Mother,

"I will now give you a more lengthened account of my proceedings than I did in my last.

"Last Saturday week I reached Ambleside, as you know. As I was following my luggage to Foxhow I met Mrs. Arnold, and visited Stockgill force.

"*Sunday.*—I did nothing particular, although it was a splendid day, and we saw the mountains beautifully.

"*Monday.*—Hard frost. We went up Lufrigg, the mountain close by Foxhow, to try if we could get any skating, but it would not bear my weight. I and Matt Arnold then went down to a swampy sort of lake to shoot snipes: we found a good number, but it came on to rain, and before we got back from Elterwater (the name of the lake) we were well wet through.

"*Tuesday—Wednesday.*—Rain—rain!

"*Thursday.*—We were determined to do something, so Matt, Tom, and I took horse and rode to Keswick, and we had a most beautiful ride. We left Lady Fleming's on the right, went along the shores of Rydale Lake, then from Rydale to Grasmere, then through the pass called High Rocae (I don't know if that is rightly spelt), leaving a remarkable mountain called the Lion and the Lamb on the right—then to Thurlmere, leaving Helvellyn on the right. Thurlmere is a beautiful little lake: there is a very fine rock on the left bank called Ravenscrag, and on the right Helvellyn rises to an immense height. Then the view of Keswick was most beautiful: Keswick straight before us—Bassenthwaite beyond Keswick in the distance; Derwentwater on our left—Saddleback and Skiddaw on the right, one 2,780 and the other 3,000 feet high, and Helvellyn (3,070 feet) behind us. It was a rainy, misty day, so that we did not see so much as we might have done, and it was only at odd moments that we caught a glimpse of Helvellyn free from clouds, but we were lucky in seeing it at all; they gave us such a dinner at the inn (without our requiring anything grand) as would have made a Southern stare—all the delicacies of the season, potted char among the rest—and charging us only 2s. apiece.

"*Friday.*—Rainy. Walked into Ambleside to see Mr. Cotton off by the mail, and afterwards as the weather cleared up we went out on Windermere, and had a very pleasant afternoon.

"*Saturday.*—A fine day. Tom and I determined to do something 'gordgeous,' and so we set out to walk up Helvellyn, and we had some precious good walking before we got up. We started from the foot at a quarter past eleven, and reached the summit at a quarter to one. One hour and a half,—pretty good walking, considering three-quarters or more was as steep or steeper than the side of Beacon Hill[1] which we slide down. Although quite warm in the valley, the top of the mountain was a sheet of ice, and the wind blew quite a gale. It did not, however, prevent us from enjoying a view of nearly fifty miles on all sides. We saw Windermere, Coniston, and the sea towards the south, as far as Lancaster. Ulswater close on the north-east; Skiddaw and Saddleback and Bassenthwaite Lake on the north; on the west the range of mountains in which is Scawfell, 3,160 feet, the highest mountain in England. We saw into Scotland, Cumberland, Cheshire, Lancashire, and Yorkshire. It was a most splendid day, but there was a sort of mist in the very far distance which prevented our seeing quite as much as we should otherwise. Helvellyn on the side towards Ulswater descends in a

---

[1] A hill in Lord Carnarvon's park at Highclere, near Newbury.

precipice 1,000 feet, and a long narrow ridge, called, I think, Straddle Edge, from its narrowness, stretches out at right angles from the mountain, on the same side. There are innumerable places in which a person might break his neck, or be frozen to death without help, as few go up the mountain at this time of the year, it being a continual frost up there. We made ourselves very comfortable under the lee of a cairn, or heap of stones, which had been raised on the very highest point, round a tall upright pole. I got up, and put a stone at the top, and we put a newspaper which contained our grub into the middle of the heap, having first taken out a quantity of stones; how long it will stay there I don't know. We then proceeded to grub with uncommon appetite,—some hard 'unleavened bread,' some tolerable cheese, and a lot of the common oat-cake they make in the country. We had some good fun, loosening and rolling masses of rock down the precipitous side into the 'Red Tarn,' a largish bit of water, and into the table-land below. We then came home by Gresdale Tarn and Grasmere, after a good long walk. This was last Saturday.

"Dr. and Mrs. Arnold are very kind, and I have spent a very pleasant week here. I go away on Tuesday to Escrick Park. Next Wednesday week, or about that time, I shall start for London again, and shall be with you about the 20th; till which time

"I remain, your affectionate son,

"G. E. Hughes.

"Love to all."

The ride to Keswick, mentioned in this letter, is alluded to also in one which I received in this last sad month of

May from one of his companions, who has allowed me to use it for your benefit. Its natural place would perhaps be at the end of this memoir, but I prefer to insert it here:—

"HARROW, *May 23rd*, 1872.

"MY DEAR HUGHES,

"I had seen so little of your brother George of late years that I seemed at first to have no business to write about his death; but now, as the days go on, I cannot resist the desire of saying a word about him, and of asking after his wife and children. Not two years ago I had a delightful day at Offley with him—the only time I ever was there; and all I saw of him then, and on the very rare occasions when we met by accident, confirmed my old remembrance of him—that he was one of the most delightful persons to be with I ever met, and that he had, more than almost anybody one met, the qualities which will stand wear. Everything about him seemed so sound; his bodily health and address were so felicitous that one thought of his moral and intellectual soundness as a kind of reflex from them; and now it is his bodily health which has given way! His death carries me back to old times, and the glory and exploits (which are now so often presented so as to bore one) of youth, and strength, and coolness, have their ideal for me in what I remember of him, and his era. His taking the easy lead at golf latterly, as he did in his old days at football and rowing, seemed to me quite affecting. Tell me about his poor wife; and what children has he left, and what are they doing?

"It will be a great loss to you too. Do you remember our ride together to Keswick some thirty-two years ago? We have all a common ground in the past. I have told Macmillan to send you a little book, of which the chief recommendation is that I believe it is the sort of book my father would have been impelled to make if he had had to do with schools for the poor. My kind regards to your wife.

" Affectionately yours,
" Matthew Arnold."

From Foxhow George went to visit another of his most intimate school friends. During that visit he gave another proof of coolness and courage of a rare kind, and also of his singular modesty. We at home only heard of what had happened through the newspapers, and never could get him to do anything more than pooh-pooh the whole affair. In fact, the first accurate description of the occurrence came to me after his death, in the letter to his sister which follows. It is written by the schoolfellow just referred to :—

"Dusseldorf, *June 4th*, 1872.

"My dear Mrs. Senior,

"Your very kind letter of the 20th May has just reached me here; and I cannot express in writing one tithe of what I feel. I had no idea of the news it had in store for me; for, having been travelling about lately, I had missed the announcement of the sad loss which we have all had; and so your letter fell on me as a thunderbolt. Poor dear old George! old in the language of affection, ever since we were all at Rugby. Oh! how much I regret now that I never found time in these last few idle years of my life to pay him a visit. And yet, to the brightness and pleasure of my recollections of him, nothing could be added. To the very last he was what he was at the very first: a giant, with a giant's gentleness and firmness. You may perhaps none of you know that he always felt sure boating was too violent an exercise for anyone. I remember well (and now how sorrowfully) one conversation in which he told me how many of the best oars had fallen in the midst of apparent health and strength. How little did I then think he was to go! and yet I recollect I carried away with me from that conversation an idea that he suspected he had heart-complaint. Was this the case?

"But I will not trouble you to write out to me abroad; for I trust I may soon return to England, and then I shall take the liberty of writing to ask you to see me at Lavender Hill.

"You ask about his stopping the horses at Escrick. It was in 1840 or 1841. He had been left with my two eldest brothers to come home last; and whilst these two brothers were calling at our York Club, George was left sitting alone in the carriage. Suddenly the driver fell off the box in a fit, upon the horses, and they started off. George remembered that in the six-mile drive home there are two right-angled turns; so he determined to get out, run along the pole, and stop the horses. The first time he tried was in vain: steadying himself with his hand on the horses' quarters, he only frightened them more; so he coolly returned into the carriage again and waited till they had lost some of their speed. He then crept through the window again; ran quicker along the pole, caught their bearing reins, turned them round, and brought back the carriage in triumph to my brothers, who were anxious enough by that time! And then the gentle modest look he had when we all praised him the next morning, I never can forget. Oh, he charmed all: a better creature never lived.

"Tell his boys from me he never could have dreamt even of any divergence from truth. As all men of power, he seemed silent and receptive rather than busy; and where you left him, you picked him up; though the interval might have been ever so long a one.

"I remain, your most sincerely,

"STEPHEN W. LAWLEY."

CHAPTER III.

A FATHER'S LETTERS.

IF this memoir is to do for you, his sons and nephews, what I hope it may, you must be told of his weak points. You have seen already that he had to leave school half a year sooner than he would otherwise have left, because he was too easy-going as a sixth-form boy, and would not exert himself to keep order; and he had a constitutional indolence, which led him to shirk trouble in small matters, and to leave things to manage themselves. This fault used to annoy your grandfather, who was always exceedingly particular as to business habits, such as answering letters, and putting things in their right places. When we first were allowed to use guns, he gave us special instructions never to bring them into the house loaded. At the end of the Christmas holidays, just after George was made a præpostor, we brought our guns in loaded, and left them in the servants' hall during luncheon. After lunch, when we went to take them out again, by some carelessness George's went off, and he narrowly escaped being shot, and the charge went through two floors. Your grandfather said nothing at the moment, but, soon afterwards, George's neglect to answer some questions on business matters produced from him the first of a series of letters, which certainly did us much good at the time, and I think may be just as useful to you. Most boys have the same kind of faults, and I cannot see that any of you need such advice less than we did.

"Three questions I put to you in recent letters. These, supposing me simply a common acquaintance, and in a position to ask the questions, should have been promptly answered, and it is but reasonable to claim what is due to any Mr. Jones or Mr. Jobson. Without self-command enough to be punctual and methodical, you cannot realize your plans as to more serious things than I now write about; nor, indeed, can you do anything *effective* in study without it. Read as much as you will, it will be like filling the sieve of the Danaids. But to drop fine metaphors and come to plain English, in heaven's name begin to be wide awake to the common exigencies and observances of life. You can see distant and abstracted things well enough; but in such common things as are understood and practised by every boy behind a counter who is worth his salt, you are in the state of a blind puppy in the straw. I do not speak with the least anger on the subject; but, as a man of common worldly sense, I cannot too pointedly and forcibly urge on you, that without a complete alteration in this respect, everything of real importance which you attempt in the business of life will be an absolute failure. You swear by Scott. Recollect Athelstan the Unready. He gives ample proof of both high valour and sound sense, and, when roused from his ruminative state, is even forcibly eloquent (where he floors the insolence of De Bracy). Yet he is the butt of the whole piece, because he is always ten minutes after time in thought and action; albeit he is by nature a finer character than Cedric, and twice as big and well-born. But everyone minds Cedric because he knows his own will and purpose, and carries it out promptly, with the power of seeing such things as are directly before his nose."

George's reply appears to have contained some statement as to his intentions in the matter of reading, as well as satisfactory answers to the neglected questions Your grandfather, however, returns to the charge again:—

"I fully believe you have every desire and intention to follow up the course I wish, though your own experience in the vacation must have shown you that this desire is not enough unless backed by determination and method. I should not wish you to debar yourself of the full portion of healthy exercise desirable at your age, which is like 'the meat and mass which hindereth no man,' as our quaint old English expresses it. But I certainly wish you to recollect that the present year" [1838—he was seventeen] "is one of the most important in your life, as you are just of the age when the character forms itself one way or the other, and when time becomes valuable in a double degree. You told me of your own accord that your wish was to distinguish yourself at Oxford. If you are as certain as I am that this wish is a wise and desirable one, the next point is, to let it become one of those determinations which are only qualified by 'Deo volente.' With the foundation which has been already laid, the thing is undoubtedly in your power, with life and health ; and, if these fail us, the fault lies not in ourselves. The secret of attaining any point is, not so much in the quantity of time bestowed on it at regular and stated intervals, as in the strong will and inclination which makes it a matter of curiosity and interest, recurring to us at odds and ends of time, and never out of the mind ; a labour of inclination rather than a matter of duty—a chase, as it were, of a wild duck" [we lived close to a river where wild ducks bred]. "instead of a walk for the promotion of health and appetite. This sort of interest anyone may create on anything he pleases : for it is an artificial taste, not perhaps so easily understood at your time of life. . . . Industry in one's vocation, when an honest and creditable one, is a Christian duty, although followed by persons indifferent to anything but self-interest. And it usually pleases God so to dispose of the course of events, that those best qualified to be useful to others in their generation have the best prospect of success in it. . . . The knowledge of history, divinity, and the dead languages, which you are now acquiring, are the basis of a liberal education, and play into each other as naturally as the hilt of a weapon fits the blade : these therefore are the points of leading interest in your life, in which your push should be made. Composition also is a valuable thing, in order to impart clearly to others what you know yourself, and prevent your candle from being hid under a bushel ; and nothing bears a higher value in the world than this faculty. Mathematics are good, as they strengthen the attention and clear the head. In these I see you took a first class, and as I think you have a turn for them, I trust you will hold your present footing without sacrificing things which hereafter may be more essential. A fair progress in modern languages is not to be neglected ; but the great points of interest are such as I have laid down, viz. knowledge of the connexion, and leading features, of sacred and profane history; a true digestion of it in your head, and the power of clearly expressing whatever thoughts arise from it; and a critical acquaintance with the original languages from which the knowledge is derived. This, I have no doubt, will correspond with Dr. Arnold's ideas as to the objects and direction of study in your case. In short, make up your mind what you will do, what you will be, and what portion of success you may fairly hope for by fairly pointing your nose to the desirable end; then keep it pointed there as steadily as the pin of the dial ('*gnomon*' if you want to be learned). And remember, that *the more irksome any habit is in its formation, the more pleasantly and satisfactorily it sticks to you when formed.* Order and clockwork in small things is what you want. *Exempli gratia*, the key of the pew-box gave us a long hunt the other day, till in going to church we found it sticking in the lock. Then, none of you ever put a book in its place again. N. S—— *does*, because he learned the habit from compulsion, and it has become second nature."

"DONNINGTON, 1839.

" Your mother and grandmother are both anxious that some destination should be early fixed for all of you; but on this I, who am more answerable, am rather cautious; feeling that much depends on what your own habits and predilections may be. At all events the right basis of every one's education is this—to love God and your neighbour, and do your duty with diligence in whatever state of life circumstances may place you. No one can live in vain acting on these principles, and whatever tends not to their establishment is of very trifling importance. I have no time to pursue the subject further at present, as this is a busy morning, and your mother will want a good share of this paper. I have begun another folio to Jack. N.B. You always have luck when I begin a letter, as I take a folio sheet in the spirit of foresight. Wat never brought his fishing-rod in; he is old enough now to cultivate orderly habits, and *eschew* (not chew) mouse pie. N.B. Eschew comes from Teutonic *schauern*, to shudder at."

Again in 1840, referring to this indolent, easy-going habit, your grandfather writes :—

"The temper of mind which I mean is often allied (and in your case I trust and believe it is) to certain qualities, good in a social and Christian sense: candour, good nature, and a contented spirit; just as certain peculiar weeds are frequently the indication of a sound and wholesome staple of soil: but then they *are* weeds, and it is a Christian duty to eradicate them in the labourer responsible for the care of the soil. In this respect the children of this world are the wisest in their generation. We may safely take examples of skill, activity, and abiding interest in a purpose, from the worst and most selfish men; and those who are wise, as well as good, do take the example, and profit by it. Not but that young persons constitutionally indolent, if they are also conscientious in their duty to their friends, and correct in the general notion that industry in a calling is a duty, do complete their stated hours of study in an honest and competent manner. And this is precisely your case; a case which has put me in an awkward position in pointing out your deficiencies. It is an ungracious thing to tease and spur a tractable, good-tempered horse, who trots his seven miles an hour of his own accord, even when you know that he has the blood and power in him to go up to the best hounds with due training, and it is hard to treat one's son worse than one's horse (or than one's servants, for your mother truly taxes me with not keeping my household tightly up to their duties). These deficiencies nevertheless exist, and are indicated by many small traits. Now, indolence in my sense, and as applied to you, is exactly in the correct sense of the word—'in' (*non*) and '*doleo*,' viz., as the Scots say, 'canna be fashed'—cannot, unless led by some moral duty, or exigence of society, jump upon my legs and go about some little, teasing, but necessary five minutes' errand, or turn my mind for the same time, by a sudden jerk, to something which breaks up the prevailing train of thought. This is a constitutional failing of my own, and I have been forced to establish rules in some things to break it through. But I never was tempted by it so as to leave anything to chance where any favourite project was concerned; *here* I expended perhaps too much accuracy and double diligence. Hence I fear the evil is more deeply seated in you. The last example is this:—On inspecting and laying up the two double guns, I found the inside of one rusty, the other black from careless cleaning. Now, no thoroughbred sportsman ever contents himself, when laying up his tools in ordinary, with trusting to his servant's care, and not his own eye, in cleaning. Yet you are a good shot—doubtless because you like shooting, and employ while in the field all the power of your mind and body to attain your purpose. What is wanting is, the submission to dry detail (*id quod dolet*). But no one can be a thorough and efficient master of anything who cannot see to details. Pump away with all your might, and welcome, but your labour will be thrown away if you won't submit to stop the leaks in your tub. It is exactly from the same temper that I have seen you take up a book in company when rather dull. True, the book is the more sensible companion, but the time and place prescribes '*quod dolet*,' though not so agreeable, or edifying. Thus it is in fifty things, all arguing a want of that order, and exactness, resulting from the due division of the mind. I could even argue it from the trifling trait of your never carrying a tassel to wipe your arrows with, and leaving your books open on the table for the maids to spill ink or dust on. I can prescribe for you in future in these respects, if you will trust yourself to me cheerfully, and not look aguish and woe-begone when spurred up to the mark by a word in season."

And again in 1842:—

"As an illustration is necessary to a theme, suppose two garden engines of equal capacity, one leaky and loosely constructed, the other well staunched, which does not waste a drop of water. You may cobble and plug up the first *pro tem.*, and by working it with a strong arm make it play well: anon it leaketh again, and without a strong and troublesome effort it is no go. The second is tight and compact at a moment's notice, and throws its stream with precision, just as much as is wanted, and where it is wanted—

φωνᾶντα συνετοῖσιν.

"I think there has been some improvement this year in your briskness and precision, but there is room for more. Straws show which way the wind blows. *Videlicet*, the not having looked in the calendar.[1] Then you keep your watch with your razors, and never can tell me what's o'clock. With respect to your capacity for giving your might and main to a subject, when you are at it, I know enough to be well satisfied, and have no criticism to make."

[1] As to sending in prize exercises at Oxford. A copy of his was too late.

The last reference of this kind which I find in your grandfather's letters, which were always carefully preserved by George, occurs in 1846. After referring to an omission to notice the transfer of some money to his account, your grandfather goes on:—

"By the bye, I certainly am under the impression that you shrink from the trouble of details and cares of this kind; the same impression which I entertained five or six years ago. You must yourself know best whether I am right or not, and it is *now* of importance that you should candidly ask yourself the question, and, if self-convicted, turn completely over a new leaf, on account of having others soon to act and manage for, as master of a house. I need hardly tell you I suppose that, in all points of paramount importance, your character has formed in a manner which has given me thorough satisfaction, and that your friends and relatives have just reason for appreciating you highly as a member of society. I will also add, and with truth, that I know no man of your age, who, if placed in a difficult situation, would in my opinion act with more sense, firmness, and discretion; and this is much indeed. But the possession of a naturally decisive and influential character is just what requires digested method in small and necessary things; otherwise the defect is more ridiculously anomalous than in a scatter-brained fellow, whom no one looks up to, or consults. It is a godsend if a beggar is any better than barefoot, but what would you say to a well-dressed man otherwise, who had forgotten his feet, and came into a drawing-room with a pair of greasy slippers? Without buttering you up, yours happens to be a character which, to round it off consistently and properly, demands accuracy in small and irksome things. In some respects

I really think you have acquired this; in others, are acquiring it; and have no doubt that when ten years older, you will have progressed in a suitable degree. Meantime, if you are conscious that anything is wanting in these respects, it is high time now to put on the steam."

As a slight illustration of the effect of these letters, I may add here, that to the end of his life, when he came in from shooting, my brother never rested until he had cleaned his gun with his own hands. When asked why he did not leave it to the keeper, he said he preferred its being done at once, and thoroughly; and the only way of being sure of that, was to do it himself. In some respects, however, he never got over his constitutional love of taking things easily, and avoiding bother and trouble.

CHAPTER IV.

OXFORD.

My brother went up to Oxford full of good resolves as to reading, which he carried out far better than most men do, although undoubtedly, after his first year, his popularity, by enlarging the circle of his acquaintance to an inconvenient extent, somewhat interfered with his studies. Your grandfather was delighted at having a son likely to distinguish himself actually resident in his own old College. In his time it had occupied the place in the University now held by Balliol. Copleston and Whately had been his tutors; and, as he had resided a good deal after taking his degree, he had seen several generations of distinguished men in the common room, including Arnold, Blanco White, Keble, Pusey, and Hampden. Moreover, there was a tradition of University distinction in his family; his father had been Seatonian Prizeman and Chancellor's Medallist at Cambridge, and he himself had carried off the Latin verse prize, and one of the English Odes recited before the United Sovereigns, when they paid a visit to the Oxford Commemoration in 1814, with Wellington, Blücher, and a host of the great soldiers of that day.

His anxiety as to George's start at Oxford manifested itself in many ways, and particularly as to the want of punctuality, and accuracy in small matters, which he had already noticed. As a delicate lesson on this subject, I find him taking advantage of the fact that George's watch was in the hands of the maker for repairs, to send him his own chronometer, adding: "As your sense of trustworthiness in little and great things is a considerably multiplied multiple of your care for your own private property (which doubtless will grow to its right proportion when you have been cheated a little), I have no doubt old Trusty will return to me in as good order as when he left me. Furthermore, it is possible you may take a fancy to him when you have learnt the value of an unfailing guide to punctuality. In which case, if you can tell me at the end of term that you have, to the best of your belief, made the most of your time, I will with great pleasure swap with you. As to what is making the best of your time, you would of course like to have my ideas. Thus, then"——and your grandfather proceeds to give a number of rules, founded on his own old Oxford experience, as to reading, and goes on :—

"All this, you will say, cuts out a tolerably full employment for the term. But when you can call this in your recollections, '*terminus alba cretâ notandus*,' it will be worth trouble. I believe the intentions of most freshmen are good, and the first term generally well spent: the second and third are often the trial, when one gets confidence in oneself; and the sense of what is right and honourable must come in place of that deference for one's superior officers, which is at first instinctive. I am glad you find you can do as you please, and choose your own society without making yourself at all remarkable. So I found, for the same reasons that facilitate the matter to you. Domestic or private education, I believe, throws more difficulties in the way of saying 'No' when it is your pleasure so to do, and the poor wight only gets laughed at instead of cultivated. After all, one may have too many acquaintance, unexceptionable though they be. But I do not know that much loss of time can occur to a person of perfectly sober habits, as you are, if he leaves wine parties with a clear head at chapel time, and eschews supping and lounging, and lunching and gossiping, and tooling in High Street, and such matters, which belong more to particular cliques than to a generally extended acquaintance in College. In all these things, going not as a raw lad, but as a man of nineteen, with my father's entire confidence, I found I could settle the thing to my satisfaction in no time: your circumstances are precisely the same, and the result will probably be the same. I applaud, and $\kappa\nu\delta\iota\zeta\epsilon$, and clap you on the back for rowing: row, box, fence, and walk with all possible sturdiness. Another thing: I believe an idea prevails that it is necessary to ride sometimes, to show yourself of equestrian rank. If you have any mind this way, write to Franklin to send Stevens with your horse; keep him a few weeks, and I will allow you a £5 note to assert your equestrian dignity, now or at any other time. This is a better style of thing than piaffing about on hired Oxford cocky-horses, like Jacky Popkin, and all such half-measures. The only objection to such doings is, that you certainly do see a style of men always across a horse who are fit for nothing else, and *non constat* that they always know a hock from a stifle-joint. But this is only *per accidens*. And if you have a fancy for an occasional freak this way, remember I was bred in the saddle, and, whatever my present opinions may be from longer experience, can fully enter into your ideas."

You will see by his answer how readily George entered into some of his father's ideas, though I don't think he ever sent for his horse. A few weeks later, in 1841, he writes :—

" Now to answer your last letters. I shall be delighted to accept you as my prime minister for the next two years. Any plan of reading which you chalk out for me I think I shall be able to pursue — at least I am sure I will try to do so. Men reading for honours now generally employ 'a coach.' If you will condescend to be my coach, I will try to answer to the whip to the best of my power."

Your grandfather accepted the post with great pleasure; and there are a number of his letters, full of hints and directions as to study, which I hope you may all read some day, but which would make this memoir too long. You will see later on how well satisfied he was with the general result, though in one or two instances he had sad disappointments to bear, as most fathers have who are anxious about their sons' work. The first of these happened this year. He was specially anxious that George should write for the Latin Verse, which prize he himself had won. Accordingly George wrote in his first year, but, instead of taking his poem himself to the Proctor's when he had finished it, left it with his College tutor to send in. The consequence was, it was forgotten till after the last day for delivery, and so could not be received. This was a sad trial to your grandfather, both because he had been very sanguine as to the result, and because here was another instance of George's carelessness about his own affairs, and want of punctuality in small things. However, he wrote so kindly about it, that George was more annoyed than if he had been very angry, and set to work on the poem for the next year as soon as the subject was announced, which I remember was "*Noachi Diluvium.*" You may be sure that now the poem went in in good time, but in due course the Examiners announced that no prize would be given for the year. I do not know that any reason was ever given for this unusual course, which surprised everyone, as it was known that several very good scholars, including, I believe, the late Head-master of Marlborough, had been amongst the competitors. Your grandfather was very much vexed. He submitted George's poem to two of his old college friends, Dean Milman and Bishop Lonsdale, both of whom had been Latin prizemen ; and, when they expressed an opinion that, in default of better copies of verses, these should have been entitled to the prize, he had them printed, with the following heading:—

"The refusal of the Official Committee of Examiners to award any prize for the Oxford Latin verse of 1842, has naturally led to a supposition that the scholarship and intelligence of the competitors has fallen short of the usual standard. Having, however, perused the following copy of verses, which are probably a fair specimen of those sent in, I am inclined to think, as a graduate and somewhat conversant with such subjects, that this discouraging inference is unfounded, and that the committee have been influenced in their discretion by some unexplained reason, involving no reflection on the candidates for the prize, as compared with those of former years."

The real fact I believe to have been, so far as George was concerned, that there were two false quantities in his verses; and though these were so palpable, as your grandfather remarked, "as to be obvious to any fifth-form boy, and plainly due to carelessness in transcription, and want of revision by a second person," the Examiners were clearly not bound to make allowances for such carelessness.

Many years after, in a letter to his sister, on some little success of her boy at Rugby, George writes :—

"I congratulate you on Walter's success. We are much more interested for our brats than we were for ourselves. I remember how miserable my poor father made himself once when I did not get a Latin Verse prize at Oxford, and how much more sorry I was for him than for myself. Anyhow, there is no pleasure equal to seeing one's children distinguish themselves—it makes one young again."

But I must return to his freshman's year at Oxford.

I have told you already that this was our first separation of any length. I did not see him from the day he went to Oxford in January until our Rugby Eleven went up to Lords, at the end of the half-year, for the match with the M.C.C. It was the first time I had ever played there, and of course I was very full of it, and fancied the match the most important event which was occurring in England at the time. One of our Eleven did not turn up, and George was allowed to play for us. He was, as usual, a tower of strength in a boys' Eleven, because you could rely on his nerve. When the game was going badly, he was always put in to keep up his wicket, and very seldom failed to do it. On this occasion we were in together, and he made a long score, but, I thought, did not play quite in his usual style; and on talking the matter over with him when we got home, I found that he had not been playing at Oxford, but had taken to boating.

I expressed my sorrow at this, and spoke disparagingly of boating, of which I knew nothing whatever. We certainly had a punt in the stream at home, but it was too narrow for oars, and I scarcely knew a stretcher from a rowlock. He declared that he was as fond of cricket as ever, but that in the whole range of sport, even including

F

hunting, there was no excitement like a good neck-and-neck boat-race, and that I should come to think so too.

At this time his boating career had only just begun, and rowing was rather at a discount at Oxford. For several years Cambridge had had their own way with the dark blues, notably in this very year of 1841. But a radical reformer had just appeared at Oxford, whose influence has lasted to the present day, and to whom the substitution of the long stroke with sharp catch at the beginning (now universally accepted as the only true form) for the short, digging "waterman's" stroke, as it used to be called, is chiefly due. This was Fletcher Menzies, then captain of the University College boat. He had already begun to train a crew on his own principles, in opposition to the regular University crew, and, amongst others, had selected my brother, though a freshman, and had taken him frequently down the river behind himself in a pair-oar. The first result of this instruction was, that my brother won the University pair-oar race, pulling stroke to another freshman of his own college.

In Michaelmas Term, 1841, it became clear to all judges of rowing that the opposition was triumphant. F. Menzies was elected captain of the O. U. B. C., and chose my brother as his No. 7, so that on my arrival at Oxford in the spring of 1842, I found him training in the University crew. The race with Cambridge was then rowed in the summer, and over the six-mile course, between Westminster and Putney bridges. This year the day selected was the 12th of June. I remember it well, for I was playing at the same time in the Oxford and Cambridge match at Lord's. The weather was intensely hot, and we were getting badly beaten. So confident were our opponents in the prowess of their University, that, at dinner in the Pavilion, they were offering even bets that Cambridge would win all three events—the cricket match, the race at Westminster, and the Henley Cup, which was to be rowed for in the following week. This was too much for us, and the bets were freely taken; I myself, for the first and last time in my life, betting five pounds with the King's man who sat next me. Before our match was over the news came up from the river that Oxford had won.

It was the last race ever rowed by the Universities over the long six-mile course. To suit the tide, it was rowed down, from Putney to Westminster Bridge. My brother unluckily lost his straw hat at the start, and the intense heat on his head caused him terrible distress. The boats were almost abreast down to the Battersea reach, where there were a number of lighters moored in mid stream, waiting for the tide. This was the crisis of the race. As the boats separated, each taking its own side, Egan. the Cambridge coxswain, called on his crew: Shadwell, the Oxford coxswain, heard him, and called on his own men; and when the boats came in sight of each other again from behind the lighters, Oxford was well ahead. But my brother was getting faint from the effects of the sun on his head, when Shadwell reminded him of the slice of lemon which was placed in each man's thwart. He snatched it up, and at the same time F. Menzies took off his own hat and gave it him; and, when the boat shot under Westminster Bridge with a clear lead, he was quite himself again.

In our college boat—of which he was now stroke, and which he took with a brilliant rush to the head of the river, bumping University, the leading boat, to which his captain, F. Menzies, was still stroke, after two very severe races—he always saw that every man had a small slice of lemon at the start, in memory of the Battersea reach.

Next year (1843), owing to a dispute about the time, there was no University race over the London course, but the crews were to meet at the Henley Regatta. The meeting was looked forward to with more than ordinary interest, as party feeling was running high between the Universities. In the previous year, after their victory in London, the Oxford boat had gone to Henley, but had withdrawn, in consequence of a decision of the stewards, allowing a man to row in the Cambridge crew who had already rowed in a previous heat, in another boat. So the cup remained in the possession of the Cambridge Rooms, a London rowing club, composed of men who had left college, and of the best oarsmen still at the University. If the Cambridge Rooms could hold the challenge cup this year also, it would become their property. But we had little fear of this, as Menzies' crew was in better form than ever. He had beaten Cambridge University in 1842, and we were confident would do it again; and, as the Rooms were never so strong as the University, we had no doubt as to the result of the final heat also. I remember walking over from Oxford the night before the regatta, with a friend, full of these hopes, and the consternation with which we heard, on arriving at the town, that the Cambridge University boat had withdrawn, so that the best men might be draughted from it into the Rooms' crew, the holders of the cup. Those only who have felt the extraordinary interest which these contests excite can appreciate the dismay with which this announcement filled us. Our boat would, by this arrangement, have to contend with the picked oars of two first-class crews; and we forgot that, after all, though the individual men were better, the fact of their not having trained regularly together made them really less formidable competitors. But far worse news came in the morning. F. Menzies had been in the Schools in the previous month, and the strain of his examination, combined with training for the race, had been too much for him. He was down with a bad attack of fever. What was to be done? It was settled at once that my brother should row stroke, and a proposal was made that the vacant place in the boat should be filled by one of Menzies' college crew. The question went before the stewards, who, after long deliberation, determined that this could not be allowed. In consequence of the dispute in the previous year, they had decided, that only those oarsmen whose names had been sent in could row in any given race. I am not sure where the suggestion came from, I believe from Menzies himself, that his crew should row the race with seven oars; but I well remember the indignation and despair with which the final announcement was received.

However, there was no help for it, and we ran down the bank to the starting-place by the side of our crippled boat, with sad hearts, cheering them to show our appreciation of their pluck, but without a spark of hope as to the result. When they turned to take up their place for the start, we turned also, and went a few hundred yards up the towing-path, so as to get start enough to enable us to keep up with the race. The signal-gun was fired, and we saw the oars flash in the water, and began trotting up the bank with our heads turned over our shoulders. First one, and then another, cried out that "we were holding our own," that "light blue was not gaining." In another minute they were abreast of us, close together, but the dark blue flag the least bit to the front. A third of the course was over, and, as we rushed along and saw the lead improved foot by foot, almost inch by inch, hope came back, and the excitement made running painful. In another minute, as they turned the corner and got into the straight reach, the crowd became too dense for running. We could not keep up, and could only follow with our eyes and shouts, as we pressed up towards the bridge. Before we could reach it the gun fired, and the dark blue flag was run up, showing that Oxford had won.

Then followed one of the temporary fits of delirium which sometimes seize Englishmen, the sight of which makes one slow to disbelieve any crazy story which is told of the doings of other people in moments of intense excitement. The crew had positively to fight their way into their hotel, and barricade themselves there, to escape being carried round Henley on our shoulders. The enthusiasm, frustrated in this direction, burst out in all sorts of follies, of which you may take this as a specimen. The heavy toll-gate was pulled down, and thrown over the bridge into the river, by a mob of young Oxonians headed by a small, decorous, shy man in spectacles, who had probably never pulled an oar in his life, but who had gone temporarily mad with excitement, and I am confident would, at that moment, have led his followers not only against the Henley constables, but against a regiment with fixed bayonets. Fortunately, no harm came of it but a few broken heads and black eyes, and the local authorities, making allowances for the provocation, were lenient at the next petty sessions.

The crew went up to London from Henley, to row for the Gold Cup, in the Thames Regatta, which had just been established. Here they met the Cambridge Rooms' crew again, strengthened by a new No. 3 and a new stroke, and the Leander, then in its glory, and won the cup after one of the finest and closest races ever rowed. There has been much discussion as to these two races ever since in the boating world, in which my brother was on one occasion induced to take part. "The Oxford University came in first," was his account, "with a clear lead of the Leander, the Cambridge crew overlapping the Leander. We were left behind at the start, and had great difficulty in passing our opponents, not from want of pace, but from want of room." And, speaking of the Henley race, which was said to have been won against a "scratch crew," he adds: "A 'scratch crew' may mean anything short of a perfectly trained crew of good materials. Anyone who cares about it will find the names of the Rooms' crew at p. 100 of Mr. Macmichael's book, and by consulting the index will be able to form a judgment as to the quality of our opponents. *We* had a very great respect for them. I never attempted to exaggerate the importance of the 'seven oars' race,' and certainly never claimed to have beaten a Cambridge University crew on that occasion." It will always remain, however, one of the most interesting of the heroic records of a noble English sport.

He announced his own triumphs at home as follows, from the Golden Cross, where the Oxford crew then stopped:—

"My dear Father and Mother,—I should have been with you yesterday, but was obliged to wait because they had not finished the gold oars which we have won at Putney. We have been as successful here as we were at Henley, and I hope I shall bring home the cup to show you. I shall be home to-morrow, and very glad to get to Donnington again. I don't feel the least unsettled by these proceedings, and am in an excellent humour for reading."

The two great cups came to Donnington, and remained for the year on your grandfather's sideboard, who could never quite make up his mind about them; pride at his son's extraordinary prowess being dashed with fears as to the possible effects on him. George himself, at this time, certainly had no idea that he was at all the worse for it, and maintained in his letters that pulling "is not so severe exercise as boxing or fencing hard for an hour." "You may satisfy yourselves I shall not overdo it. I have always felt the better for it as yet, but if I were to feel the least inconvenience I should give it up at once."

One effect the seven-oar race had on our generation at Oxford: it made boating really popular, which it had not been till then. I, amongst others, was quite converted to my brother's opinion, and began to spend all my spare time on the water. Our college entered for the University four-oar races in the following November Term, and, to my intense delight, I was selected for No. 2, my brother pulling stroke.

Our first heat was against Balliol, and through my awkwardness it proved to be the hardest race my brother ever rowed. At the second stroke after the start I caught a crab (to use boating phrase), and such a bad one that the head of our boat was forced almost into the bank, and we lost not a stroke or two, but at least a dozen, Balliol going away with a lead of two boats' lengths and more. Few strokes would have gone on in earnest after this, and I am not sure that my brother would, but that it was my first race for a University prize. As it was, he turned round, took a look at Balliol, and just said, "Shove her head out! Now then," and away we went. Of course I was burning with shame, and longing to do more than my utmost to make up for my clumsiness. The boat seemed to spring under us, but I could feel it was no doing of mine. Just before the Gut we were almost abreast of them, but, as they had the choice of water, we were pushed out into mid stream, losing half a boat's length, and having now to pull up against the full current while Balliol went up on the Oxford side under the willows. Our rivals happened also to be personal friends, and I remember well becoming conscious as we struggled up the reach that I was alongside, first of their stroke, the late Sir H. Lambert, then of No. 3, W. Spottiswoode, and at last, as we came to the Cherwell, just before the finish, of our old schoolfellow, T. Walrond, who was pulling the bow oar. I felt that the race was won, for they had now to come across to us; and won it was, but only by a few feet.

I don't think the rest of us were much more distressed than we had been before in college races. But my brother's head drooped forward, and he could not speak for several seconds. I should have learnt then, if I had needed to learn, that it is the stroke who wins boat races.

Our next heat against University, the holders of the cup was a much easier affair. We won by some lengths, and my brother had thus carried off every honour which an oarsman can win at the University, except the sculls, for which he had never been able to enter. I cannot remember any race in which he pulled stroke and was beaten.

There are few pleasanter memories in my life than those of the river-side, when we were training behind him in our college crew. He was perhaps a thought too easy, and did not keep us quite so tightly in hand as the captains of some of the other leading boats kept their men. But the rules of training were then barbarous, and I think we were all the better for not being strictly limited even in the matter of a draught of cold water, or compelled to eat our meat half cooked. He was most judicious in all the working part of training, and no man ever knew better when to give his crew the long Abingdon reach, and when to be content with Iffley or Sandford. At the half-hour's rest at those places he would generally sit quiet, and watch the skittles, wrestling, quoits, or feats of strength which were going on all about. But if he did take part in them, he almost always beat everyone else. I only remember one occasion on which he was fairly foiled. In consequence of his intimacy with F. Menzies, our crew were a great deal with that of University College, and much friendly rivalry existed between us. One afternoon one of their crew,[1] R. Mansfield, brother of George's old vaulting antagonist, rode down to Sandford, where, in the field near the inn, there was always a furze hurdle for young gentlemen to leap over. In answer to some chaffing remark, Mansfield turned round, and, sitting with his face towards his horse's tail, rode him over this hurdle. Several of us tried it after him, George amongst the number, but we all failed; and of course declared that it was all a trick, and that his horse was trained to do it under him, and to refuse under anybody else.

The four-oar race was the last of my brother's boating triumphs. At the end of the term he gave up rowing, as his last year was beginning, and he was anxious to get more time for his preparation for the Schools. I am not sure that he succeeded in this as, strong exercise of some kind being a necessity to him, he took to playing an occasional game at cricket, and was caught and put into the University Eleven. He pulled, however, in one more great race, in the Thames Regatta of 1845, when he was still resident as a bachelor, attending lectures. Number 6 in the Oxford boat broke down, and his successor applied to him to fill the place, to which he assented rather un-

[1] Author of "The Log of the Water Lily," &c.

willingly. The following extract from a letter to his father gives the result, and the close of his boating career:—

"You will have seen that Oxford was unsuccessful in London for the Grand Cup, but I really think we should have won it had it not been for that unlucky foul. I only consented to take an oar in the boat because they said they could not row without me, and found myself well up to the work."

He always retained his love for rowing, and came up punctually every year to take his place on the umpire's boat at the University race, to which he had a prescriptive claim as an old captain of the O.U.B.C. And this chapter may fitly close with a boating song, the best of its kind that I know of, which he wrote at my request. It appeared in Mr. Severn's "Almanac of English Sports," published at Christmas 1868. I had rashly promised the editor to give him some verses for March, on the University race, and put it off till it was time to go to press. When my time was limited by days, and I had to sit down to my task in the midst of other work, I found that the knack of rhyming had left me, and turned naturally to the brother who had helped me in many a copy of verses thirty years back. I sent him down some dozen hobbling lines, and within a post or two I received from him the following, on the March Boat Race:—

The wood sways and rocks in the fierce Equinox,
   The old heathen war-god bears rule in the sky,
Aslant down the street drives the pitiless sleet,
   At the height of the house-tops the cloud-rack spins by.

Old Boreas may bluster, but gaily we'll muster,
   And crowd every nook on bridge, steamboat, and shore,
With cheering to greet Cam and Isis, who meet
   For the Derby of boating, our fête of the oar.

"Off jackets!"—each oarsman springs light to his seat,
   And we veterans, while ever more fierce beats the rain,
Scan well the light form of each hardy athlete,
   And live the bright days of our youth once again.

A fig for the weather! they're off! swing together!
   Tho' lumpy the water and furious the wind,
Against a "dead noser"[1] our champions can row, Sir,
   And leave the poor "Citizens" panting behind.

"Swing together!" The Crab-tree, Barnes, Chiswick are past;
   Now Mortlake—and hark to the signaling gun!
While the victors, hard all, long and strong to the last,
   Rush past Barker's rails, and our Derby is won.

Our Derby, unsullied by fraud and chicane,
   By thieves-Latin jargon, and leg's howling din—
Our Derby, where "nobbling" and "roping" are vain,
   Where all run their best, and the best men must win.

No dodges we own but strength, courage, and science;
   Gold rules not the fate of our Isthmian games;
In brutes—tho' the noblest—we place no reliance;
   Our racers are men, and our turf is the Thames.

---

[1] "Dead noser," the Tyne phrase for a wind in your teeth.

The sons of St. Dennis in praise of their tennis,
  Of chases and volleys, may brag to their fill;
To the northward of Stirling, of golf, and of curling,
  Let the chiels wi' no trousers crack on as they will.

Cricket, football, and rackets—but hold, I'll not preach,
  Every man to his fancy—I'm too old to mend—
So give *me* a good stretch down the Abingdon reach,
  Six miles every inch, and " hard all " to the end.

Then row, dear Etonians and Westminsters, row,
  Row, hard-fisted craftsmen on Thames and on Tyne,
Labuan,[1] New Zealand, your chasubles[2] peel, and
  In one spurt of hard work, and hard rowing, combine.

Our maundering critics may prate as they please
  Of glory departed and influence flown—
Row and work, boys of England, on rivers and seas,
  And the old land shall hold, firm as ever, her own.

---

[1] The Bishops were famous oarsmen. Dr. Macdougal rowed bow oar in Menzies' boat, and was a dear friend of my brother's.

[2] Query: Do Bishops wear "chasubles?"— G. E. H. [Note appended by my brother to the original copy.]

CHAPTER V.

DEGREE.

THE Schools were now very near ahead of him, and, though not much behindhand with his work, considering the intensity of his exertions in other directions, he was anxious to make the most of the months that were left. He read very hard in vacation, but, when term began again, had to encounter unusual difficulties. His father's half-hinted warnings against a large acquaintance proved prophetic. In fact, I used to wonder how he ever got his reading done at all, and was often not a little annoyed with many of my own contemporaries, and other younger men still, even to the last batch of freshmen, whose fondness for his society was untempered by any thought of examinations, or honours. Not one of them could give a wine, or a breakfast party, without him, and his good-nature kept him from refusing when he found that his presence gave real pleasure. Then he never had the heart to turn them out of his rooms, or keep his oak habitually sported; and when that most necessary ceremony for a reading man had been performed, it was not respected as it should have been. My rooms were on the same staircase, half a flight below his (which looked into the quadrangle, while mine looked out over the back of the College), so that I could hear all that happened. Our College lectures were all over at one. It was well for him if he had secured quiet up to that hour; but, in any case, regularly within a few minutes after the clock had struck, I used to hear steps on the stairs, and a pause before his oak. If it was sported, kicking or knocking would follow, with imploring appeals, "Now, old 'un" (the term of endearment by which he went in College), "do open—I know you're in—only for two minutes." A short persistence seldom failed; and soon other men followed on the same errand, "for a few minutes only," till it was time for lunch, to which he would then be dragged off in one of their rooms, and his oak never get sported again till late at night. Up to his last term in College this went on, though not to quite the same extent; and even then there was one incorrigible young idler, who never failed in his "open sesame," and wasted more of my brother's time than all the rest of the College. But who could be angry with him? He was one of the smallest and most delicate men I ever saw, weighing about 8st. 10lb., a capital rider, and as brave as a lion, though we always called him "the Mouse." Full of mother wit, but utterly uncultivated, it was a perfect marvel how he ever matriculated, and his answers, and attempts at construing, in lecture were fabulous—full of good impulse, but fickle as the wind; reckless, spendthrift, fast, in constant trouble with tradesmen, proctors, and the College authorities. But no tradesman, when it came to the point, had the heart to "court," or proctor to rusticate him; and the Dean, though constantly in wrath at his misdeeds, never got beyond warnings, and "gating." So he held on, until his utter, repeated, and hopeless failure to pass his "smalls," brought his college career to its inevitable end. Unfortunately for my brother's reading, that career coincided with his third year, and his society had an extraordinary fascination for the Mouse. The perfect contrast between them, in mind and body, may probably account for this; but I think the little man had also a sort of longing to be decent and respectable, and, in the midst of his wildest scrapes, felt that his intimacy with the best oar and cricketer in the College, who was also on good terms with the Dons, and paid his bills, and could write Greek verses, kept him in touch with the better life of the place, and was a constant witness to himself of his intention to amend, some day. They had one taste in common, however, which largely accounted for my brother's undoubted affection for the little " ne'er do weel," a passion for animals. The Mouse kept two terriers, who were to him as children, lying in his bosom by night, and eating from his plate by day.

Dogs were strictly forbidden in College, and the vigilance of the porter was proof against all the other pets. But the Mouse's terriers defied it. From living on such intimate terms with their master, they had become as sharp as undergraduates. They were never seen about the quadrangles in the day-time, and knew the sound and sight of dean, tutor, and porter, better than any freshman. When the Mouse went out of College, they would stay behind on the staircase till they were sure he must be fairly out in the street, and then scamper across the two quadrangles, and out of the gate, as if their lives depended on the pace. In the same way, on returning, they would repeat the process, after first looking cautiously in at the gate to see that the porter was safe in his den. But after dusk they were at their ease at once, and would fearlessly trot over the forbidden grass of the inner quad, or sit at the Provost's door, or on the Hall steps, and romp with anybody not in a master's gown. So, even when his master's knock remained unanswered, Crib's or Jet's beseeching whine and scratch would always bring my brother to the door. He could not resist dogs, or children.

I have always laid my brother's loss of his first class at the door of his young friends, but chiefly on the Mouse, for that little man's delinquencies culminated in the most critical moment of the Schools. The Saturday before paper work began he had seduced George out for an evening stroll with him, and of course took him through a part of the town which was famous for town-and-gown rows. Here, a baker carrying a tray shouldered the Mouse into the gutter. The Mouse thereupon knocked the baker's tray off his head. The baker knocked the little man over, and my brother floored the baker, who sat in the mud, and howled "Gown, gown." In two minutes a mob was on them, and they had to retreat fighting, which, owing to the reckless pugnacity of his small comrade, was an operation that tried all my brother's coolness and strength to the utmost. By the help, however, of Crib, who created timely diversions by attacking the heels of the town at critical moments, he succeeded in bringing the Mouse home, capless, with his gown in shreds, and his nose and mouth bleeding, but otherwise unhurt, at the cost to himself of a bad black-eye. The undergraduate remedies of leeches, raw beef-steak, and paint were diligently applied during the next thirty-six hours, but with very partial success; and he had to appear in white tie and bands before the Examiners, on the Monday morning, with decided marks of battle on his face. In the evening, he wrote home:—

"MY DEAR FATHER,
 "The first day of paper work is over; I am sorry to say that I have not satisfied myself at all. Although logic was my strongest point as I thought, yet through nervousness, or some other cause, I acquitted myself in a very slovenly

manner; and I feel nervous and down-hearted about the remainder of the work, because I know that I am not so strong on those points as I was in logic. I feel inclined myself to put off my degree, but I should like to know what you think about it; I could certainly get through, but I do not think I should do myself any credit, and I am sure I should not satisfy myself. I shall continue at the paper work till I hear from you. I should be very willing to give up any plans which I have formed for the vacation, and read quietly at home; and I am sure I could put the affair beyond a doubt with a little more reading. But if you think I had better get rid of it at once, I will continue. I am in very good health, only, as I tell you, nervous and out of spirits.

"Yours affectionately,
"G. E. HUGHES."

His nervousness was out of place, as I ascertained afterwards from his tutor that the Examiners were very much pleased with his paper work. Indeed, I think that he himself soon got over his nervousness, and was well satisfied with his prospects when his turn came for *vivâ voce* examination. I was foolish enough to choose the same day for sitting in the Schools, a ceremony one had to perform in the year preceding one's own examination. It involved attendance during the whole day, listening to the attack of the four experts in row at the long table, on the intellectual works of the single unfortunate, who sat facing them on the other side. This, when the victim happens to be your brother, is a severe and needless trial of nerves and patience.

For some time, however, I was quite happy, as George construed his Greek plays capitally, and had his Aristotle at his finger ends. He was then handed on to the third Examiner, who opened Livy and put him on somewhere in the bewildering Samnite wars, and, when he had construed, closed the book as if satisfied, just putting him a casual question as to the end of the campaign, and its effect on home politics at Rome. No answer, for George was far too downright to attempt a shot; and, as he told me afterwards, had not looked at this part of his Livy for more than a year. Of course other questions followed, and then a searching examination in this part of the history, which showed that my brother knew his Arnold's Rome well enough, but had probably taken up his Livy on trust, which was very nearly the truth. I never passed a more unpleasant hour, for I happened to be up in this part of Livy, and, if the theories of Mesmerism were sound, should certainly have been able to inspire him with the answers. As it was, I was on the rack all the time, and left the Schools in a doleful state of mind. I felt sure that he must lose his first class, and told the group of our men so, who gathered in the Schools quadrangle to see the Honours list posted. The Mouse, on the other hand, swore roundly that he was certain of his first, offering to back his opinion to any amount. I did not bet, but proved to be right. His name came out in the second class, there being only five in the first; and we walked back to Oriel a disconsolate band; the Mouse, I really believe, being more cast down than any of the party. I never told him that in my opinion he was himself not a little responsible.

He was obliged to take his own name off the books shortly afterwards, and started for the Cape, leaving Crib and Jet, the only valuable possession I imagine that he had in the world, to my brother. They were lovingly tended to a good old age. Their old master joined the Mounted Rifles, in which corps (we heard at second hand, for he never wrote a letter) he fully maintained his character for fine riding and general recklessness, till he broke down altogether, and died some two years later. It is a sad little history, which carries its own moral.

CHAPTER VI.

START IN LIFE.

My brother, after taking his degree, remained up at Oxford in lodgings, attending lectures; and, when I went out of College in the term before my own examination, I joined him, and once again we found ourselves living in a common sitting room. I think it was a very great pleasure to both of us; and as soon as my troubles in the Schools were over, and the short leisure time which generally follows that event had set in, we began to talk over subjects which had hitherto been scarcely mentioned between us, but which, on the threshold of active life, were becoming of absorbing interest. In the previous autumn I had made a tour with a pupil in the North of England and Scotland. I had gone, by choice, to commercial hotels in several of the large northern towns, as I had discovered that commercial rooms were the most likely places for political discussion, and was anxious to talk over the great question of that day with the very vigorous and able gentlemen who frequented them. The Anti-Corn-Law agitation was then at its height, and, to cut a long story short, I had come back from the North an ardent Freetrader. In other directions also I was rapidly falling away from the political faith in which we had been brought up. I am not conscious, indeed I do not believe, that Arnold's influence was ever brought to bear directly on English politics, in the case even of those boys who (like my brother and myself) came specially under it, in his own house, and in the sixth form. What he did for us was, to make us think on the politics of Israel, and Rome, and Greece, leaving us free to apply the lessons he taught us in these, as best we could, to our own country. But now his life had been published, and had come like a revelation to many of us; explaining so much that had appeared inexplicable, and throwing a white light upon great sections, both of the world which we had realized more or less through the classics, and the world which was lying under our eyes, and all around us, and which we now began, for the first time, to recognize as one and the same.

The noble side of democracy was carrying me away. I was haunted by Arnold's famous sentence, "If there is one truth short of the highest for which I would gladly die, it is democracy without Jacobinism;" and "the People's Charter" was beginning to have strange attractions for me.

It was just one of those crises in one's life in which nothing is so useful, or healthy, for one, as coming into direct and constant contact with an intellect stronger than one's own, which looks at the same subjects from a widely different standpoint.

Now, in the Anti-Corn-Law agitation the leaders of the League were in the habit of using very violent language. Their speeches were full of vehement attacks on the landlords and farmers of England, and of pictures of country life as an inert mass of selfishness, tyranny, and stupidity. My brother's hatred of exaggeration and unfairness revolted against all this wild talk; and his steady appeal to facts known to us both often staggered my new convictions. On the general economical question, imperfectly as I understood it, I think I often staggered him. But, on the other hand, when he appealed to the example of a dozen landlords whom I knew (including your grandfather), and made me look at the actual relations between them and their tenants and their labourers, and ask myself whether these statements were not utterly untrue in their case and in the county we knew; whether they were not probably just as untrue of other counties; and, if that were so, whether a cause which needed such libels to support it could be a just one, I was often in my turn sadly troubled for a reply.

Again, though Arnold's life influenced him quite as powerfully as it did me, it was in quite a different direction, strengthening specially in him the reverence for national life, and for the laws, traditions, and customs with which it is interwoven, and of which it is the expression. Somehow, his natural dislike to change, and preference for the old ways, seemed to gain as much strength and nourishment from the teaching and example of our old master, as the desire and hope for radical reforms did in me. As for democracy, not even Arnold's dictum could move him. " The Demos " was for him always, the fatuous old man, with two oboli in his cheek, and a wide ear for the grossest flatteries which Cleon or the Sausage-seller could pour into it. Those of you who have begun Aristophanes will know to what I allude. Now, if he had been a man who had any great reverence for rank or privilege, or who had no sympathies with or care for the poor, or who was not roused to indignation by any act of oppression or tyranny, in the frame of mind I was in I should have cared very little for anything he might have urged. But, knowing as I did that the fact was precisely the reverse—that no man I had ever met was more indifferent to rank and title, more full of sympathy and kindliness to all below him, or more indignant at anything which savoured of injustice—I was obliged to admit that the truth could not be all on my side, and to question my own new faith far more carefully than I should have done otherwise.

And so this was the last good deed which he did for me when our ways in life parted for the first time, and I went up to London to read for the Bar, while he remained at Oxford. His plans were not fixed beyond the summer. He had promised to take two or three Oriel men to Scotland on a reading party, and accordingly went with them to Oban in July; and, while there, accepted an offer, which came to him I scarcely know how, to take charge of the sons of the late Mr. Beaumont at Harrow, as their private tutor.

I must own I was much annoyed at the time when I heard of this resolution. I could see no reason for it, and many against it. Here was he, probably the most popular man of his day at Oxford, almost sure of a fellowship if he chose to stay up and read for it, one of the best oars and cricketers in England, a fine sportsman, and enjoying all these things thoroughly, and with the command of as much as he chose to take of them, deliberately shelving himself as the tutor of three young boys. I am afraid there was also a grain of snobbishness at the bottom of my dislike to the arrangement. Private tutors were looked upon then by young men—I hope it is so no longer—as a sort of upper servants; and I was weak enough, notwithstanding my newly acquired liberalism, to regard this move of George's as a sort of loss of caste. He was my eldest brother, and I was very fond and proud of him. I was sure he would distinguish himself in any profession he chose to follow, while there was no absolute need of his following any; and it provoked me to think of his making what I thought a false move, and throwing away some of the best years of his life.

However, I knew it was useless to remonstrate, as he had

made up his mind, and so held my tongue, and came to see that he was quite right. It was not till nearly three years later, when his engagement was over and he had entered at Doctors' Commons, that I came to understand and appreciate his motives. The first of these you may gather from the following extract from a letter of your grandfather's, dated February 23rd, 1849 :—" George, it seems, is unusually lively at the idea of going tooth and nail to work with men instead of boys; and, now that he has for three years gratified his whim of keeping himself wholly off my hands, consents to be assisted like his brothers." This "whim" of proving to his own satisfaction that he was worth his keep, and could make his own living, is not a very usual one nowadays, when most young Englishmen seem to assume that they have a natural right to maintenance at the expense of some one. He had then six other brothers, on whom the example was not altogether thrown away, though none of us were ever able quite to come up to it. It had the effect, however, of making us thoughtful in the matter of expenditure; and, consequently, of the four who went to the universities, and two who entered the army, not one got into any money difficulties.

But George had other motives for this step besides the "whim" of independence. He wished for leisure to make up his mind whether he should take holy orders, as he had at one time intended to do. And, since leaving Rugby, he had had no time either for the study of modern languages or for general reading, and he was anxious to make up his arrears in both of these directions. This engagement would give him the leisure he wanted, while keeping him at regular routine work. His resolve, though taken at the risk of throwing himself back some years in his future profession, whatever that might be, was thoroughly characteristic of him, and owing, I think, in great measure to your grandfather's own precepts. He was fond of telling us family stories, and there was none of these of which he was more proud than that of his maternal great-grandmother. This good lady was the widow of George Watts, Vicar of Uffington, a younger son himself, who died at the age of forty-two, leaving her in very poor circumstances. She sold off everything, and invested the proceeds in stocking a large dairy farm in the village where she had lived as the great lady, there being no resident squire in the parish. If any of you ever care to make a pilgrimage to the place, you will find the farmhouse, which she occupied nearly 200 years ago, close to the fish-pond in Uffington. She was well connected, and her friends tried to persuade her not to give up her old habits; but she steadily refused all visiting, though she was glad to give them a cup of chocolate, or the like, when they chose to call on her. By attending to her business, rising early and working late, she managed to portion her daughter, and give her son a Cambridge education, by which he profited, and died Master of the Temple, where you may see his monument. He was true to his mother's training, and sacrificed good chances of further preferment, by preaching a sermon at Whitehall before George II. and his mistress, on Court vices, on the text, "And Nathan said unto David, Thou art the man." Such stories, drunk in by a boy of a quiet, self-contained, thorough nature, were sure to have their effect; and this "whim" of George's was one of their first-fruits in his case. I must add, that there is no family tradition which I would sooner see grow into an article of faith with all of you than this of thriftiness, and independence, as points of honour. So long as you are *in statu pupillari*, of course you must live at the expense of your friends; but you may do so either honestly, or dishonestly. A boy, or young man, born and bred a gentleman, ought to feel that there is an honourable contract between him and his friends; their part being to pay his bills, and make him such an allowance as they can afford, and think right, and sufficient; his, to work steadily, and not to get in debt, or cultivate habits and indulge tastes which he cannot afford. You will see through life all sorts of contemptible ostentation and shiftlessness on every side of you. Nurses, if they are allowed, begin with fiddle-faddling about children, till they make them utterly helpless, unable to do anything for themselves, and thinking such helplessness a fine thing. Ladies' maids, grooms, valets, flunkeys, keepers, carry on the training as they get older. Even at public schools I can see this extravagance and shiftlessness growing in every direction. There are all sorts of ridiculous expenses, in the shape of costumes and upholstery of one kind or another, which are always increasing. The machinery of games gets every year more elaborate. When I was in the eleven at Rugby, we "kept big-side" ourselves; that is to say, we did all the rolling, watering, and attending to the ground. We chose and prepared our own wickets, and marked out our own creases, for every match. We had no "professional" and no "pavilion," but taught ourselves to play; and when a strange eleven was coming to play in the school close, asked the Doctor for one of the schools, in which we sat them down to a plain cold dinner. I don't say that you have not better grounds, and are not more regularly trained cricketers now; but it has cost a great deal in many ways, and the game has been turned into a profession. Now, one set of boys plays just like another; then, each of the great schools had its own peculiar style, by which you could distinguish it from the rest. And, after you leave school, you will find the same thing in more contemptible forms, at the Universities and in the world. You can't alter society, or hinder people in general from being helpless, and vulgar—from letting themselves fall into slavery to the things about them if they are rich, or from aping the habits and vices of the rich if they are poor. But you may live simple manly lives yourselves, speaking your own thought, paying your own way, and doing your own work, whatever that may be. You will remain gentlemen so long as you follow these rules, if you have to sweep a crossing for your livelihood. You will not remain gentlemen in anything but the name, if you depart from them, though you may be set to govern a kingdom. And whenever the temptation comes to you to swerve from them, think of the subject of this memoir, of the old lady in the farmhouse by Uffington fish-pond, and the tablet in the Temple Church.

Such a resolution as that which, as I have just shown you, was taken by my brother at the end of his residence at Oxford, is always a turning-point in character. If faithfully and thoroughly carried out, it will strengthen the whole man; lifting him on to a new plane, as it were, and enabling him, without abruptly breaking away from his old life, to look at its surroundings from a higher standpoint, and so to get a new and a truer perspective. If repented of, or acted out half-heartedly, it is apt to impair a man's usefulness sadly, to confuse his judgment, and soften the fibre of his will. He gets to look back upon his former pursuits with an exaggerated fondness, and to let them gradually creep back, till they get a stronger hold on him than ever, so that he never learns to put them in their right place at all. The moral of which to you boys is—think well over your important steps in life, and, having made up your minds, never look behind. George never did. From Oban he writes home: "My forthcoming engagement occupies all my thoughts, and indeed a good deal of my time; for if I intend to succeed, I must be well up in everything. I shall not, therefore, be able to make many excursions from Oban." Your grandfather had been a friend of Sir Walter Scott, and had brought us up on his works; and had suggested to George that this would be a good opportunity for visiting a number of the spots immortalized by the Wizard of the North. This was his answer.

In the same spirit I find him writing about the same time as to a new cricket club, which was starting under very favourable auspices in Berkshire, and in which he had been asked to take a leading part: "I shall certainly not join the A. C. Club; and as for Tom, I should think his joining more improbable still. Cricket is over for both of us, except accidentally."

In this spirit he took to his new work; and, going into it heartily and thoroughly, found it very pleasant. He occupied Byron House at Harrow, with his pupils, in which his old friend Mr. M. Arnold afterwards lived. There were several of his old schoolfellows, and college friends, among the Masters; and I, and others of his old friends, used to run down occasionally, on half-holidays, from London, and play football or cricket with the boys, amongst whom the prestige of his athletic career of course made him a great favourite and hero.

Thus he got as much society as he cared for, and found time, in the intervals of his regular work, for a good deal of general reading. In fact, I never knew him more cheerful than during these years of what most of us regarded as lost time, and in which we certainly expected he would have been bored, and disappointed. This would not have been so perhaps had he proved unsuccessful; but his pupils got on well in the school, and their father soon found him out, and appreciated him. At the beginning of the first long vacation he writes home:—

"Mr. Beaumont, finding I am fond of a gun, has most kindly offered me a week's shooting on his moors. I could easily manage it, and meet you in London in time to visit Lady Salusbury. You will not think, I know well, that I like shooting better than home; and if you would like to see me before you go to London, pray say so, and the moors will not occupy another thought in my head. It is not everyone who would have taken the trouble to find out that I liked shooting, and I feel Mr. Beaumont's kindness; in fact, he seems as generous as a prince to everyone with whom he has anything to do."

But it was in his own family, where he would have wished for it most, that the reward came most amply. He became in these years the trusted adviser of your grandfather on all family matters, and especially with respect to his three youngest brothers. The direction of their education was indeed almost handed over to him, and nothing could exceed the admiration and devotion with which they soon learnt to regard him. The eldest of them was sent to Harrow in 1848 to be under his eye, and you may judge of the sort of supervision he exercised by this specimen of his reports:—

"I think he has been suffering the usual reaction which takes place when a boy goes to a new school. He worked hard at first, and then, finding he had a good deal of liberty and opportunity of amusement, grew slack. He is too fond of exercise to be naturally fond of work, as some boys are who are blessed with small animal spirits; and he is not yet old enough to see clearly the object of education, and the obligation of work. I have no doubt he will very soon find this out; but, if not, it will very soon be forced on his notice by the unpleasantness of being beaten by his contemporaries."

Speaking of his letters of advice to the boys, your grandfather writes:—

"They have given me at least as much pleasure as them. You are doing a very kind thing in the most judicious way, and have assisted the stimulus which they required. Good leaders make a steady-going team, and allow the coachman to turn round on his box. Arthur [the youngest] will in his turn benefit by these fellows, I doubt not. You would, I think, be pleased to see how naturally he takes to cricket. In fact, take him altogether, he is a very good specimen of a six-year-old."

But perhaps nothing will show you in a short space what he was to his younger brothers so well as one of their own letters to him, and one of his to your grandmother. The first is from your uncle Harry, written almost at the end of his first half at Rugby:—

"My dear George,

"I am very much obliged to you for writing such a capital letter to me the other day, and for all your kind advice, which you may be sure is not entirely thrown away. I remember all the kind advice you gave me last winter, as we were coming from skating at Benham. You warned me from getting into 'tick,' and you said you were sure I should be able to act upon your good advice, and from that moment I determined not to go on tick, without I could *possibly help*. I haven't owed a penny to anyone this half-year, and I don't mean to owe anybody anything in the money way; and I have not spent all my money yet, and if I have not got enough to last me till the end of the half-year, I am *determined* not to tick; and I *heartily thank God* that I have elder brothers to guide me and advise me; I am afraid I should have done badly without them. You advised me also in your kind letter to work steadily. I fancy I am placed pretty decently; the form I am in is the upper remove. I keep low down in my form, principally from not knowing my Kennedy's grammar. I find it very hard to say by heart. I should have been placed higher, I think, if I had known it; and I should advise Arthur to begin it now, if he is coming to Rugby, which I hope he is. He will find it disagreeable now, but he would find it worse if he did not know it when he came here. I think if you would be kind enough to write to him, and show him how necessary it is for him to learn it, he would be only too glad to do it. I think the great fault in me is, not so much forgetfulness, but a not having a determination to do a thing at the moment. I put it off. But I have, I am sorry to say, innumerable other faults. Mamma sent me a book of prayers, which I read whenever I have got time, and I say my prayers every night and morning, and I pray for all of you. I have now mentioned, I think, everything that you seemed anxious about in your letter."

The next letter is dated two years later, when the question what profession the writer of the last was to follow, had become important:—

"DEAREST MOTHER,

"I will answer your questions as well as I am able. Harry will not lower himself by farming. It might have been so ten years ago, but the world is getting less absurd, and, besides, I think more gentlemen are now taking it up as a profession (Mr. Huxtable, for instance, and many others), and are most highly respected. But to succeed in farming in England now, one must be a remarkable man; one must thoroughly understand all practical details, and be able to work oneself better than a labourer; besides this, the farmer must be a tolerable chemist and geologist, must understand bookkeeping and accounts, and must be enterprising and yet cautious; as patient as Job, and as active minded (and bodied) as anyone you can think of. Now Harry, although amiable, is rather indolent, and unless he can entirely get rid of this, he will ruin himself in a year by farming in England. In Ireland or the colonies it might be different. For the same reasons I would not recommend the Bar for Harry. It is very laborious, the confinement great, and it requires a hard head: moreover, the education is quite as expensive as an Oxford one, if that is any consideration. However, if you think that Harry can acquire (not an ordinary, but) an extraordinary amount of diligence, let him come to the Bar or farm. I confess I should discourage both ideas. If you can get a cadetship for him, I would certainly accept it. The two dangers of Indian military life are extravagance and dissipation, and I don't think Harry inclined to either. He has not been extravagant at Rugby, and the temptations of a public school are as great as they are anywhere; and I think he is well-principled and kind-hearted, which will save him from the other danger. The army is getting much better, and officers begin to find out that they may do immense good in their profession by looking after the condition of their men. If you should obtain a cadetship, it will not be difficult to make Harry understand that he will have other duties besides drill, and I believe he would perform them. I am sure he would be exceedingly popular with officers and men. If he had been bad-tempered, or disobedient, or ill-conditioned, I should have recommended the navy, as by far the best school for such a character; but as he does not want such discipline, as we have no interest, as it is a poor profession in a worldly point of view, and as he is (I fancy) rather too old, I think it is out of the question. I confess I should hesitate much between orders and the army. If I saw any likelihood of Harry's doing anything at Oxford, I should like to see him a clergyman. I am sure he would be a conscientious one, and therefore happy. But I *don't* think he would do anything (though of course he would pass), and there are the same temptations there as in the army. On the whole, I would try immediately to procure a cadetship; if you cannot get one, I would try to induce Harry to take orders. I said something about Ireland and the colonies in connection with farming. On second thoughts, I don't think Harry would be a suitable person. Amiable tempers always require (at first) some one to look up to and lean upon; they are longer in learning to stand alone. Now, no one is so much isolated as a colonist. He is thrown entirely on his own resources, and has no one to give him advice and sympathy. In the army, and indeed in orders, one is generally trained to bear responsibility. So I am for the cadetship. He will be at once provided for, and will return to England in the prime of life with a competence. This is always supposing that he will escape the dangers of the profession (as I think), and that you and he do not think the advantages counterbalanced by the separation. I have no doubt that when communication with India is easier (and it will soon be incredibly easier), officers will come home at shorter intervals."

Meantime he was studying the same question carefully in his own case, with a view to determining whether he should take orders when his work at Harrow was over. His father and mother, though on the whole wishing that he should do so, were perfectly content to let him think the matter out, and settle it his own way. They seem, however, to have supplied him with specimens of contemporary pulpit literature, upon some of which he comments in his correspondence, not, on the whole, with any enthusiasm. "Surely," he sums up some criticism on a popular preacher of that day, "there is a pulpit eloquence equally remote from fine writing and familiarity, such as was Dr. Arnold's. I am doubtful as to reading these books, for I know that I ought not to think of the style, and yet I cannot help it. It takes me down against my will."

Your grandfather replied: "The Church ought certainly

to be a labour of love, and followed with zeal. If on a final review of your sentiments, aided perhaps by the advice of some clergyman you look up to (why not Vaughan ?) you do not think you could engraft this zeal on sound convictions, and an upright character, you are quite right in deciding for the Bar. In after life you will not be wholly dependent on a profession, and many of our best men have started as late."

In the end he made up his mind against taking orders, but not on any of the grounds which deter so many young men of ability now. "My only objection," he writes to his mother, "to taking orders is, that it might not suit me. Once ordained, it is impossible to change your profession; and unless a man has his whole soul in this profession, he is useless, or worse."

And so, at the end of his three years at Harrow, he resolved to go to the Bar, and choosing that branch of it for which his previous reading had best qualified him, took his degree of Doctor of Civil Law, and entered at Doctors' Commons.

You will have recognized by this time how carefully your grandfather watched the development of character in his sons, and that he was by no means inclined to overlook their faults, or to over-estimate their good qualities. The longer I live myself, the more highly I am inclined to rate his judgment of men and things, and this is the conclusion he had formed at this time of his eldest son's character. It occurs in a letter to a relative then living, and dated 25th January, 1849 :—

"I am glad you have had an opportunity (difficult to get from his reserved character) of seeing what is in George when put to the proof. There are many men of his age with more active benevolence and habits of more general utility, as well as perhaps warmer spiritual feeling, also more useful acquired knowledge. His great *forte* rather lies in those qualities which give men the ascendency in more troubled times—perfect consistency of word and purpose, great moral and physical courage, and a scrupulous sense of what is due to oneself and others in the relations of social life, combined with the caution a man should possess, who never intends to retract an opinion or a profession. Much perhaps of the *chevalier sans tache* who used to be the fashion in the rough times before steam and 'ologies came in. In my time these sort of people were always more popular among Oxford youngsters (who are very acute in reading character) than mere wits, scholars, or dashing men. I suppose it is so still, and thereby account for the estimation which it seems he had in Oriel. And I apprehend this sort of established character must help a man in a profession where he means to work, and I will answer for his doing so."

But there is one feature in George's character which this estimate of it does not bring out. I mean his great unselfishness. As an illustration of this, I will show you how he treated a proposal made on account of your grandfather while he was at Harrow. We had had the first loss in our circle. Your uncle Walter, whom none of you remember, a young officer in the

Artillery, had died of an attack of yellow fever in British Guiana. This had shaken your grandfather a good deal, and his health was no longer strong enough to allow him to follow, and enjoy, his country pursuits. Besides, the house at Donnington was too big for the shrunken family which now gathered there, and those of us who had flitted were settled, or likely to settle, in London. So it was thought that it would be well for your grandfather, and all of us, if he were to follow, and move up to the neighbourhood of town. In any case George's opinion would have been the first taken on such a step, but in this it was necessary that he should consent, as Donnington was settled on him. He was very much attached to the place in which we had all grown up; and local, and county, and family associations had a peculiarly strong hold on him. But all these were set aside without a second thought. All he was anxious about was, that so serious a change should be well considered. "I think," he writes to his mother, "you should be cautious about changing. In the first place, it will cause you personally an immense amount of annoyance, which you ought never to incur, especially now. Then you will miss your garden, and your village occupations, and your neighbours. My last letter might have led you to suppose that I myself preferred Hampstead to Donnington, but that is not the case. I should consider it desirable under certain circumstances. If you and my father, and Jeanie and the rest, think these circumstances exist, I sincerely hope you will change, and lose no time about it. But do not do a thing which will cause you a great deal of trouble and annoyance without the clearest grounds. Above all, believe, and this I say with the most perfect truth, that I shall be equally happy whichever you do."

CHAPTER VII.

1849-50 :—*AN EPISODE.*

AT the time when my brother's Harrow engagement came to an end, I had just settled in a London house, and, to my great delight, he proposed to come and live with us, and occupy our spare room in Upper Berkeley Street. Besides all my other reasons for rejoicing at this arrangement, which you may easily imagine for yourselves when you have read thus far, there was a special one just at this time, which I must now explain. The years 1848-9 had been years of revolution, and, as always happens at such times, the minds of men had been greatly stirred on many questions, and specially on the problem of the social condition of the great mass of the poor in all European countries. In Paris, the revolution had been the signal for a great effort on the part of the workmen; and some remarkable experiments had been made, both by the Provisional Government of 1848, and by certain employers of labour, and bodies of skilled mechanics, with a view to place the conditions of labour upon a more equitable and satisfactory footing; or, to use the common phrase of the day, to reconcile the interests of capital and labour. The Government experiment of "national workshops" had failed disastrously, but a number of the private associations were brilliantly successful. The history of some of these associations—of the sacrifices which had been joyfully made by the associates in order to collect the small funds necessary to start them—of the ability and industry with which they were conducted, and of their marvellous effect on the habits of all those engaged in the work—had deeply interested many persons in England. It was resolved to try an experiment of the same kind here, but the conditions were very different. The seed there had already taken root amongst the industrial classes, and the movement had come from them. Here the workpeople, as a rule, had no belief in association except for defensive purposes. It was chiefly amongst young professional men that the idea was working, and it was necessary to preach it to those whom it most concerned. Accordingly a society was formed, chiefly of young barristers, under the presidency of the late Mr. Maurice, who was then Chaplain of Lincoln's Inn, for the purpose of establishing associations similar to those in Paris. It was called the Society for Promoting Working Men's Associations, and I happened to be one of the original members, and on the Council. We were all full of enthusiasm and hope in our work, and of propagandist zeal: anxious to bring in all the recruits we could. I cannot even now think of my own state of mind at the time without wonder and amusement. I certainly thought (and for that matter have never altered my opinion to this day) that here we had found the solution of the great labour question ; but I was also convinced that we had nothing to do but just to announce it, and found an association or two, in order to convert all England, and usher in the millennium at once, so plain did the whole thing seem to me. I will not undertake to answer for the rest of the Council, but I doubt whether I was at all more sanguine than the majority. Consequently we went at it with a will: held meetings at six o'clock in the morning (so as not to interfere with our regular work) for settling the rules of our central society, and its offshoots, and late in the evening, for gathering tailors, shoemakers, and other handicraftsmen, whom we might set to work ; started a small publishing office, presided over by a diminutive one-eyed costermonger, a rough and ready speaker and poet (who had been in prison as a Chartist leader), from which we issued tracts and pamphlets, and ultimately a small newspaper ; and, as the essential condition of any satisfactory progress, commenced a vigorous agitation for such an amendment in the law as would enable our infant Associations to carry on their business in safety, and without hindrance. We very soon had our hands full. Our denunciations of unlimited competition brought on us attacks in newspapers and magazines, which we answered, nothing loth. Our opponents called us Utopians and Socialists, and we retorted that at any rate we were Christians; that our trade principles were on all-fours with Christianity, while theirs were utterly opposed to it. So we got, or adopted, the name of Christian Socialists, and gave it to our tracts, and our paper. We were ready to fight our battle wherever we found an opening, and got support from the most unexpected quarters. I remember myself being asked by Mr. Senior, an old friend of your grandfather, to meet Archbishop Whately, and several eminent political economists, and explain what we were about. After a couple of hours of hard discussion, in which I have no doubt I talked much nonsense, I retired, beaten, but quite unconvinced. Next day, the late Lord Ashburton, who had been present, came to my chambers and gave me a cheque for £50 to help our experiment; and a few days later I found another nobleman, sitting on the counter of our shoemakers' association, arguing with the manager, and giving an order for boots.

It was just in the midst of all this that my brother came to live with us. I had already converted him, as I thought. He was a subscribing member of our Society, and dealt with our Associations; and I had no doubt would now join the Council, and work actively in the new crusade. I knew how sound his judgment was, and that he never went back from a resolution once taken,

and therefore was all the more eager to make sure of him, and, as a step in this direction, had already placed his name on committees, and promised his attendance. But I was doomed to disappointment. He attended one or two of our meetings, but I could not induce him to take any active part with us. At a distance of twenty-two years it is of course difficult to recall very accurately what passed between us, but I can remember his reasons well enough to give the substance of them. And first, as he had formerly objected to the violent language of the leaders of the Anti-Corn-Law agitation, so he now objected to what he looked upon as our extravagance. "You don't want to divide other people's property?" "No." "Then why call yourselves Socialists?" "But we couldn't help ourselves: other people called us so first." "Yes; but you needn't have accepted the name. Why acknowledge that the cap fitted?" "Well, it would have been cowardly to back out. We borrow the ideas of these Frenchmen, of association as opposed to competition as the true law of industry; and of organizing labour—of securing the labourer's position by organizing production and consumption—and it would be cowardly to shirk the name. It is only fools who know nothing about the matter, or people interested in the competitive system of trâde, who believe, or say, that a desire to divide other people's property is of the essence of Socialism."
" That may be very true: but nine-tenths of mankind, or,

at any rate, of Englishmen, come under one or the other
of those categories. If you are called Socialists, you will
never persuade the British public that this is not your
object. There was no need to take the name. You have
weight enough to carry already, without putting that on
your shoulders." This was his first objection, and he
proved to be right. At any rate, after some time we
dropped the name, and turned the "Christian Socialist"
into the "Journal of Association." And English Socialists
generally have instinctively avoided it ever since, and
called themselves ' co-operators," thereby escaping much
abuse in the intervening years. And, when I look back,
I confess I do not wonder that we repelled rather than
attracted many men who, like my brother, were inclined
theoretically to agree with us. For I am bound to admit
that a strong vein of fanaticism and eccentricity ran
through our ranks, which the marvellous patience, gentleness, and wisdom of our beloved president were not enough
to counteract, or control. Several of our most active and
devoted members were also strong vegetarians, and phonetists. In a generation when beards and wide-awakes
were looked upon as insults to decent society, some of
us wore both, with a most heroic indifference to public
opinion. In the same way, there was often a trenchant,
and almost truculent, tone about us, which was well
calculated to keep men of my brother's temperament at
a distance. I rather enjoyed it myself, but learnt its

unwisdom when I saw its effect on him, and others, who were inclined to join us, and would have proved towers of strength. It was right and necessary to denounce the evils of unlimited competition, and the falsehood of the economic doctrine of "every man for himself;" but quite unnecessary, and therefore unwise, to speak of the whole system of trade as "the disgusting vice of shop-keeping," as was the habit of several of our foremost and ablest members.

But what really hindered my brother from taking an active share in our work was not these eccentricities, which soon wore off, and were, at the worst, superficial. When he came to look the work fairly in the face, he found that he could not heartily sympathise with it; and the quality of thoroughness in him, which your grandfather notices, would not let him join half-heartedly. His conclusion was reached somehow in this way: "It comes to this, then. What you are all aiming at is, the complete overthrow of the present trade system, and the substitution of what, you say, will prove a more honest and righteous one. It is not simply a question of setting up, and getting a legal status for, these half-dozen associations of tailors and shoemakers, and these grocery stores. If the principle is good for anything, it must spread everywhere, and into every industrial process. It can't live peaceably side by side with the present system. They are absolutely antagonistic, and the one must cast out the other. Isn't that so?" I, of course, could not deny the conclusion. "Well, then," his argument went on, "I don't see my way clearly enough to go on. Your principle I can't object to. It certainly seems truer, and stronger, and more in accord with Christianity, than the other. But, after all, the business of the world has always gone on upon the other, and the world has had plenty of time to get to understand its own business. You may say the results are not satisfactory, are proofs that the world has done nothing but blunder. It may be so: but, after all, experience must count for something, and the practical wear and tear of centuries. Self-interest may be a low motive, but the system founded upon it has managed somehow, with all its faults, to produce a very tolerable kind of world. When yours comes to be tried practically, just as great abuses may be found inseparable from it. You may only get back the old evils under new forms. The long and short of it is, I hate upsetting things, which seems to be your main object. You say that you like to see people discontented with society as it is, and are ready to help to make them so, because it is full of injustice, and abuses of all kinds, and will never be better till men are thoroughly discontented. I don't see these evils so strongly as you do; don't believe in heroic remedies; and would sooner see people contented, and making the best of society as they find it. In fact, I was born and bred a Tory, and can't help it."

I remember it all very vividly, because it was a great

grief to me at the time, chiefly because I was very anxious to have him with us; but, partly, because I had made so sure of getting him that I had boasted of it to our Council, which included several of our old school and college friends. They were delighted, knowing what a valuable recruit he would prove, and now I had to make the humiliating confession, that I had reckoned without my host. He continued to pay his subscription, and to get his clothes at our tailors' association till it failed, which was more than some of our number did, for the cut was so bad as to put the sternest principles to a severe test. But I could see that this was done out of kindness to me, and not from sympathy with what we were doing.

But my disappointment had at least this good result, that it opened my eyes thoroughly, and made me tolerant of opposition to my own most earnest, and deepest, convictions. I have been what I suppose would be called an advanced Liberal ever since I was at Oxford, but have never been able to hate or despise the old-fashioned Tory creed; for it was the creed of almost the kindest, and bravest, and ablest man I have ever known intimately—my own brother.

I must, however, add here, that he always watched with great interest the social revolution in which he could not take an active part. In 1851, the Industrial and Provident Societies' Act, under which the co-operative societies of different kinds first obtained legal recognition, was passed, chiefly owing to the exertions of Mr. Ludlow and other members of our old Council. There are now more than 1,000 societies registered under that Act in England alone, doing a yearly business of ten millions, and owning property of the amount of £2,500,000 and upwards ; and as he saw the principle spreading, and working practically, and, wherever it took root, educating the people in self-control, and thrift, and independence, he was far too good an Englishman not to rejoice at, and sympathise with, the result, though I doubt whether he ever quite got over the feeling of distrust and anxiety with which he regarded even a peaceful, and apparently beneficent, revolution.

You all know how much I wish that you should take a thorough and intelligent interest, and, in due time, an active part, in public affairs. I don't mean that you should adopt politics as a profession, because, as matters stand in this country, poor men, as most of you will be, are not able, as a rule, to do this and retain their independence. But I want you to try to understand politics, and to study important questions as they arise, so that you may be always ready to support, with all the influence you may happen to have, the measures and policy which you have satisfied yourselves will be best for your country. Of course I should like to see you all of my own way of thinking; but this is not at all likely to happen, and I care comparatively little whether you turn out Liberals or Tories, so that you take your sides conscientiously, and hold to them through good and evil report ; always remembering, at the same time, that those who are most useful and powerful in supporting a cause, are those who know best what can be said against it; and that your opponents are just as likely to be upright and honest men as yourselves, or those with whom you agree. My brother's example taught me this, and I hope it may do as much for you.

There is a little poem of Lowell's, which brings out so well the contrast between the two forces constantly at work in human affairs, and illustrates so beautifully the tempers which should underlie all action in them, that I am sure you will thank me for quoting it here. It is called "Above and Below:"—

ABOVE.

I.

O dwellers in the valley land,
  Who in deep twilight grope and cower,
Till the slow mountain's dial-hand
  Shortens to noon's triumphant hour—
While ye sit idle, do ye think
  The Lord's great work sits idle too,
That light dare not o'erleap the brink
  Of morn, because 'tis dark with you?

Though yet your valleys skulk in night,
  In God's ripe fields the day is cried,
And reapers, with their sickles bright,
  Troop, singing, down the mountain-side:
Come up, and feel what health there is
  In the frank Dawn's delighted eyes,
As, bending with a pitying kiss,
  The night-shed tears of earth she dries.

The Lord wants reapers : oh, mount up,
  Before Night comes, and cries "Too late!"
Stay not for taking scrip or cup,
  The Master hungers while ye wait;
'Tis from these heights alone your eyes
  The advancing spears of day may see,
Which o'er the eastern hill-tops rise
  To break your long captivity.

BELOW.

II.

Lone watcher on the mountain height!
  It is right precious to behold
The first long surf of climbing light
  Flood all the thirsty east with gold :
But we, who in the twilight sit,
  Know also that the day is nigh,
Seeing thy shining forehead lit
  With his inspiring prophecy.

Thou hast thine office : we have ours :
  God lacks not early service here,
But what are thine eleventh hours
  He counts with us as morning cheer;
Our day for Him is long enough,
  And when He giveth work to do,
The bruisèd reed is amply tough
  To pierce the shield of error through.

But not the less do thou aspire
  Light's earlier messages to teach,
Keep back no syllable of fire—
  Plunge deep the rowels of thy speech.
Yet God deems not thine aëried flight
  More worthy than our twilight dim—
For brave obedience, too, is Light,
  And following that is finding Him.

CHAPTER VIII.

ITALY.

THE pleasure of having my brother as an inmate was scarcely dimmed by this disappointment, and he remained with us until the autumn of 1850, a white nine months in my life. Your grandfather wrote of him a year later, when he had engaged himself to be married: " I cannot exactly fancy George a married man, seeing that to the latest period his ways in this house have been precisely the same as when he was a Rugby boy—as few wants, and as little assumption, though I have exhorted him to swagger and order a little." And, as it was at Donnington, so it had been in our diminutive town-house; indeed, I doubt whether any one of you, or any public school boy, would give so little trouble. He read hard, starting with me every morning directly after breakfast; went into no society, except that of a few old friends, and allured me away occasionally on summer afternoons, from law, and the reform of trade, to a game of cricket with the Hampstead club, of which he had become a member, or in the

Harrow playing-fields, where he was always more than welcome.

After the long vacation of 1850 he had intended to begin practice in Doctors' Commons, but was delayed by an accident. He was struck in the eye by a spent shot, in cover shooting, and, though the accident proved not to be a serious one, he was ordered to rest his eyes entirely, and accordingly settled to spend the winter in Italy. The vexation of such a check at the opening of his professional career, was almost compensated, I think, by the delight which this tour gave him. He had never been abroad at this time, except for a few days in France, and his education and natural tastes peculiarly fitted him for enjoying Italy thoroughly, for he was passionately fond of art, as well as a fine classical scholar. having never dropped his Latin and Greek, as most of us are so apt to do the moment we have taken our degrees.

He lingered a little in France, on his way south, chiefly to accustom his ear and tongue to the language, and he writes :—

"MARSEILLES, *December 6th*, 1850.

"I have not made much progress in French; everyone speaks English except the *ouvriers*. I address a waiter in a splendid sentence, which I expect will strike him with awe, and impress him with my knowledge of the French language, and he takes me down by answering in English; as much as to say, 'For goodness' sake speak your own language, and I shall understand you better.' In such a state of things, one can only listen to the conversation of Frenchmen with one another, and try to imitate their accent. In spite of beard and mustachios, it is *Voilà les Anglais* wherever we go. The only person who passes for a Frenchman is one of our American fellow-travellers, who has grown a most venerable beard; but, as he pronounces French just as if it were English, and calls Dijon '*Dee John*,' he is afraid to open his mouth for fear of being convicted as an impostor immediately. I think an Englishman's walk betrays him; I think there is an unconscious swagger about it, which savours strongly of 'ros-bif,' and which the French detect in a moment. However, they are most polite and obliging, and I think they would be glad to do you any service."

In Italy, he went from city to city, revelling in picture galleries and studios, as his eyes regained strength; taking lessons in Italian, visiting spots of historical interest, and sympathising with, and appreciating, the Italians, while wondering at their patience under the yoke of their Governments. It was the same winter which Mr. Gladstone spent in Italy, and signalized by his pamphlet on the political prisoners at Naples. Fortunately for my brother, he found Mr. Senior and his family at Naples, and again at Rome, and through their kindness, and that of Lady Malcolm, saw as much of Italian society as he cared for. A few selections from his letters will show you how he spent his time, and the impressions which his Italian travel left on his mind :—

"NAPLES, *January* 7, 1851.

"There is a party of street-singers, and a Punch, outside under my window, who distract me horribly. They have an eternal tune here, which every ragged boy sings; it is called, I believe, '*Io ti voglio*,' and is rather pretty, but you may have too much of a good thing. The beggars are most amusing, and certainly work very hard in their vocation. There is an old woman who lies on the ground in a fit all day long; another elderly female stands by her in a despairing attitude, to draw attention to her protracted sufferings, and receive the contributions of the credulously benevolent. But the old lady is nothing to a boy, who lies on the ground and bellows like a bull positively for three or four hours together; I quite admire the energy with which he follows his profession. From the number of crippled and deformed persons one sees, I am inclined to believe that the Neapolitans purposely mutilate themselves in order to succeed better in their favourite calling. They will do anything sooner than work usefully. Punch and the singers have gone, and I am at peace. All that I see of continental countries makes me more glad that I am an Englishman. None of them seem secure. The poor Pope is kept at Rome by the French; and here they say the King is very unpopular, except with the lowest class. This consciousness of insecurity makes them very suspicious and harsh. Two or three days ago an Italian, the legal adviser to our Embassy, was popped into prison on suspicion of correspondence with Mazzini. Fancy Queen Victoria putting an Englishman into Newgate on her own authority for receiving a letter from a Chartist. I suppose they are obliged to be harsh to prevent revolutions; thank Heaven, England is free and loyal."

"NAPLES, *January* 13, 1851.

"I have discovered a cousin on board the English war steamer: he is one of the midshipmen, and on Thursday I took a boat to pay him a visit. I was obliged to obtain permission from the police to go on board. There are a quantity of miserable refugees lying concealed in Naples, watching their opportunity to get on board the English ship, where they are safe under the protection of our flag. Four are on board already, but there are two police-boats constantly on the look-out near our ship, to prevent more from coming. Is it not a miserable state of things?"

"ROME, *January* 1851.

"MY DEAREST MOTHER,

". . . . Tell my father that I have been very extravagant. I have bought a copy in marble of the Psyche in the Museum at Naples; a very clever artist is executing it for me, and it will be finished about the middle of April. Mr. Senior is also having a copy taken. I do not know if my father knows the statue. It is attributed to Praxiteles. Nothing has pleased me so much, except perhaps the Dying Gladiator; and as it is very simple, the cost of the copy is comparatively trifling. It will look very well against the dark oak of your drawing-room at Donnington, and I hope you will approve of my taste."

"ROME, *January* 28, 1851.

"We saw two things yesterday which will interest you: the catacombs in which the early Christian martyrs were buried, and in which the Christians met during the persecutions to worship God. They are immense subterranean passages, extending, they say, twenty miles; but you can only see a part, as they are closed, for fear of affording shelter to thieves. The other thing was, a little church about two miles from Rome, on the Appian Road, to which a beautiful legend is attached. It is said that St. Peter, during the persecution in which he suffered martyrdom, lost heart, and fled from Rome by the Appian Road; he had arrived at the spot where the church now stands, when our Lord appeared to him, going towards Rome. The Apostle exclaimed in astonishment, 'Lord, whither goest thou?' The answer was, 'I go to Rome to be crucified again.' Whereupon Peter turned back, and re-entered the city, and suffered the death which had been predicted for him. There is no reason why this should not be true, but, true or not, it is a beautiful story, and I was much interested by it. They show a stone with the impression of our Lord's feet upon it, which is kept as a relic."

"*February* 10, 1851. — I think that my Italian progresses favourably. My master tells me that I *pronounce* it better than any other of his pupils; and as he is very strict, and finds fault with everything else, I suppose I must believe that he speaks the truth."

"*February* 18, 1851.—You will be glad to hear that I have returned to Rome from my walking tour without having been robbed, or murdered; but, indeed, I must repeat, that the good gentleman your informant must have been dreaming. We received nothing but kindness and civility, and I believe that *you* might walk along the same mountain paths with equal safety. As for us, we looked much too rough a lot to tempt robbers, being rather like banditti ourselves. One of my companions wore a venerable beard, and I am afraid we both looked picturesque ruffians. Our other companion looked tame, and carried an umbrella. We used to take a cup of coffee and a roll soon after sunrise, then walk to some romantic village about ten miles off, and there breakfast. Our breakfast consisted of an omelette, a *frittata* as they call it here, which we cooked ourselves. We used to rush into an *osteria di cucina* in a state of ravenous hunger. ——, my friend with the beard, who is a very good cook, seizes the frying-pan, I beat up the eggs, and S—— is degraded into scullion, to cut up some ham and an onion!! I believe the people think us mad. They could not conceive why we liked to cook our own breakfast, and walk when we might have ridden. After breakfast, it was so hot that we used to select a convenient spot on the hill-side, and lie down for an hour, and then continue our walk till about sunset, when we reached our resting-place for the night. In this way we saw some of the most beautiful country you can imagine. Every little exertion we made in climbing a rock was amply rewarded by something most strange and picturesque. The towns are particularly striking, some of them being built on the very top of mountains nearly 3,000 feet high, and reached with difficulty, by a narrow winding path. I am convinced that a walking tour is the only plan of really seeing Italian scenery. I made some sketches, but am sorry to say that, coming into Rome on Saturday night, my pocket was picked of my sketch-book (a very useless prize to anyone but the owner, and perhaps you), so I lost them all. I am excessively vexed, for I wanted to show you the sort of places where we took our mid-day's rest. Tivoli was our last stage, and perhaps the most interesting,—there is such a splendid waterfall there. Even if I do not see Turin, I shall be quite satisfied with my recollections of it."

After this he hastened home, meeting with no more serious adventure than the one recorded in a letter to the same correspondent, as follows:—

"I travelled from Chambery to Lyons all alone in a *coupée* with an Italian lady! Horrid situation! and what made it worse was, that the poor thing was very tired this morning, and fell fast asleep, and whilst in a state of oblivion, dropped her head comfortably on to my arm.

After revolving in my mind this alarming state of things, I thought it would be best to feign to be asleep myself; and accordingly, when we jolted over a gutter, and she awoke with a start, she found me with my eyes shut, and snoring. I hope I acted it well, but could hardly help laughing. I shortly afterwards rubbed my eyes and awoke, and she gave me a roll and some chocolate, for which I was very thankful; so I suppose she approved of my conduct."

He returned entirely restored to health, and so good an Italian scholar, that he was able to write fluently in the language, and to dedicate the little objects of art, which he brought home as presents, in appropriate verse.

One of these was an inkstand in the shape of an owl, now very common, which he presented to Lady Salusbury, a kinswoman of your grandfather, to whose adopted daughter he had lately engaged himself, with this inscription:—

> "' La stolidezza copresi talvolta di sembiante
> Savio; siccome per dar ricovero all' inchiostro
> Si fodera con piombo la civelta di bronzo
> Immago dell' uccello di sapienza.'
>
> "Ecco la finta pompa dell' uccello!
> Il quale, sotto 'l grave e savio viso
> Avendo pur di piombo il cervello
> Fra i tutti poi commuove il forte riso—
>
> "Così si trova dal sembiante bello
> Talvolta lo bel spirito diviso,
> Si trova con la roba da Dottore
> Di piombo pur la testa, ed anch' il cuore."

To the young lady herself he wrote on his return: "I have continued writing a journal, and you will be astonished to hear that your name is not once mentioned in it. It is, however, written in invisible ink across every page. It may be absurd, but I consider my feelings towards you so sacred, that I should not like to parade them even to my nearest relations."

CHAPTER IX.

MIDDLE LIFE.

On his return from his Italian tour my brother at once commenced practice in the Ecclesiastical Courts, and took a small house in Bell Yard, Doctors' Commons, where he went to reside, and which he describes to his mother as follows:—

"*April* 1851.—I am in excellent health and spirits. I have a funny little house here: there are three floors and two rooms on each: then there is a ground-floor, the front room of which I use as an office, and the back room as a bath room, for I stick diligently to the cold-water system. A kitchen below completes my establishment. I have a housekeeper, who sits downstairs in the kitchen and sleeps in the top story; she is miraculously clean and tidy, and cooks very well, although I never dine at home. She is also a wonderful gossip."

Here he practised for a few years regularly, and with very fair success, but his professional career was destined to be short and broken, and need not detain us. It is his home life with which we are concerned, and it was the pressure of what he looked upon as a higher home duty which decided him, after a struggle, to abandon his profession. He was married in the autumn of 1852, and, in the course of a few years, the health of his wife's mother by adoption made it desirable that they should be always with her, and that she should spend the winter months abroad. When it became clear that this was necessary, he accepted it, and made the best of it; though I find abundant traces in his correspondence of the effort which it required to do so. Thus he writes from Pau, the place fixed upon for their foreign winter residence, "I always found that changing one's residence and plans gave one a fit of the blues for a time, sometimes longer, sometimes shorter." And again: "The business of life is to be bored in all directions. You must not imagine, however, that I am ill, or out of spirits. I have no right to be either, and won't be, please God." But the necessary want of regular employment, the sinking into what is called "an idle man," and abandoning all active part in "the struggle for existence," was no small trial to one who held that the "full employment of all powers, physical, mental, and spiritual, is the true secret of happiness, so that no time may be left for morbid self-analysis." You are all perhaps too young to understand this, and probably, when you think about such matters at all, imagine that the happiest life must be one in which you would only have to amuse yourselves. It may, I hope, shake any such belief to find that the period in my brother's life in which he was thus thrown on his own resources, and had the most complete liberty to follow his own fancies, was just that in which you may find traces of *ennui*, and a tendency to be dissatisfied with the daily task of getting through time.

He took the best course of getting rid of the blues, however, by throwing himself heartily into such occupations as were to be had at Pau. The chief of these was a Pen and Pencil Club, to which most of the English and American residents belonged, and of which he became the secretary. Besides the ordinary meetings, for which he wrote a number of *vers de société*, on the current topics and doings of the place, the Club indulged in private theatricals. On these occasions he was stage manager, and frequently author; most of the charades and short pieces, which you have seen, and acted in, at Offley, were originally written by him for the Pen and Pencil Club at Pau. "It was a mild literary society," an old friend writes to me, "which he carried almost entirely on his own shoulders, and made a success." Then he set to work for the first time to cultivate in earnest his talent for music, and took to playing the violoncello, communicating intelligence of his own progress, and of musical doings at Pau generally, to his sister, whom he looked upon as his guide and instructress. These were not always devoid of incident, as for instance the following:—

"PAU, VILLA SALUSBURY.

"We have an opera here this season. The *prima donna* and the tenor are good; the rest so-so. The orchestra and chorus bad; the basso execrable: when he doesn't bellow like a bull, he neighs like a horse; however, he does his best. I don't know how you feel, but to me a mediocre opera is an unmitigated bore. I would rather by half hear a good French play. There was a scene at the opera the other night. The conductor of the orchestra is the *amant* of the contralto. Just before the opera began, the conductor in a jealous fit tried to strangle the contralto: whereupon the basso profundo knocked the conductor down: whereupon the conductor ran off towards the river to drown himself: whereupon he was knocked down again to save his life: whereupon he threatened to cut everybody's throat: whereupon he was locked up in prison, and there remains. So there is no conductor, and the contralto can't sing from the throttling."

The violoncello soon grew to be a resource, and I believe he played really well, though he used to groan to me as to the impossibility of adapting adult fingers to the work, and to mourn over the barbarism of our school days, when no one ever thought of music as a possible study for boys. Soon, however, other objects of deeper interest began to gather round him. His eldest boy was born in 1853, his second in 1855, during their summer in England.

"The young one," he writes to his sister, "is like his mamma, they say, and is going to be dark, which will be a good contrast to Herbert, who is a regular Saxon. I want his (Herbert's) yellow hair to grow long that it may be done into a pigtail; I think it would look quaint and create a sensation among the Cockneys, but I'm afraid I shan't get my own way. To return to the new arrival, you will be happy to hear that he inherits your talent for music; he is always meandering with his hands as if he was playing the violoncello; it is a positive fact, I assure you, and makes me laugh to bursting point. A—— must have been more struck with my performances than I had credited. I feel quite flattered to possess an infant phenomenon who played (or would have played) the violoncello, if we had let him, from his birth. In the meantime that instrument has been somewhat neglected by me. A——, the baby, and the partridges (what a conjunction), divide my allegiance. However, my music mania is as strong as ever, in spite of the rather excruciating tones which all beginners draw from the instrument: they tell me that the sounds resemble the bellowings of a bereaved cow; luckily the house is a large one."

He took to farming also, as another outlet for superfluous energy, but without much greater success than generally falls to the lot of amateurs. Indeed, his long winter absences from England kept him from gaining anything more than a superficial knowledge of agriculture, such as is disclosed in the following note to his mother, in answer to inquiries as to crops and prospects :—

"Farming is better certainly this year than the last, but we farmers always grumble, as you know, and I don't like to say anything until the new wheat is threshed. You ought to sow your tares and rye immediately, and they will do very well after potatoes; they ought to be well manured. If you mean by 'rye' Italian rye-grass, I don't exactly know when it is best to sow it; in the spring I believe, but I have never had any yet, and you must ask about it. One thing I know, that it ought to have liquid manure, to be put on directly after cutting; this will give you a fresh crop in a little more than a month."

When the Volunteer movement began, he threw himself into it at once; for no man was more impatient of, or humiliated by, the periodical panics which used to seize the country. He helped to raise a corps in his own neighbourhood, of which he became captain, and went to one of the first classes for Volunteers at the School of Musketry, to make himself competent to teach his men. As to the result he writes:—

"UNDERCLIFF, 1860.

" Our schooling at Hythe terminated on Friday last, on which day 100 lunatics were let loose upon society. I say lunatics, because all of us just now have but one idea, and talk, think, and dream of nothing but the rifle (call it Miss Enfield) morning, noon, and night. Colonel Welsford, the chief instructor, is a charming man and a delightful lecturer, and withal a greater lunatic than any of us—just the right man in the right place. 1 shot fairly, but did not distinguish myself as Harry did."

I spoke of his "*vers de société*" just now, and in this connection will here give you a specimen of them. The expenses of the corps of course considerably exceeded the Government grant, and the deficiency had to be met somehow. My brother started a theatrical performance in the Town Hall, Hitchin, as a method at once of making both ends meet, and of interesting the townspeople in the corps. The last piece of the entertainment was one of his own. The characters were played chiefly by members of his own family. He himself acted the part of a pompous magistrate, and at the close spoke the following

EPILOGUE.

" Silence in Court! what's this unseemly rumpus?
Attention to the parting words of Bumpus.
Tired of disguise, of borrowed rank and station,
Thus in a trice I work my transformation.
His wig and nose removed, the beak appears
A simple officer of Volunteers,
Who to himself restored, and sick of mumming,
Begs leave to thank you each and all for coming,
Spite of cross roads, dark lanes, tenacious clay,
And benches not too soft, to hear our play.
Next, to those friends my warmest thanks are due
Who give their aid to-night, but chief to you
Who for my sake, and only for to-day,
O'ercome your natural shyness of display.
Now comes the hardest portion of my task,
A most momentous question 'tis to ask.
I pause for your reply with bated breath—
I humbly hope you've not been bored to death?
Thanks for the signal which success assures;
Welcome to all, but most to amateurs.
Thanks, gentle friends, your welcome cheers proclaim
We have not altogether missed our aim.
Not ours your hearts to thrill, your tears to move,
With Hamlet's madness, Desdemona's love.
We dare not bid in high heroic strain

Wolsey or Richelieu rise and breathe again.
We walk in humbler paths, and cannot hope
(To quote the spirit-stirring verse of Pope)
'To wake the soul with tender strokes of Art,
To raise the genius and to mend the heart;
To make mankind in conscious virtue bold,
Live o'er each scene and be what they behold.'
No—with deep reverence for these nobler views,
We seek not to instruct you, but amuse ;
To make you wiser, better, we don't claim—
To make you laugh, our only end and aim.
And as the test of everything, men say,
Is just this simple question—does it pay ?
Well, then (I speak for self and comrades present),
This acting pays us well ; we find it pleasant.
If at the same time it amuses you,
We reap a double gain vouchsafed to few,
To please ourselves and please our neighbours too.
Besides, to-night in more material sense,
It pays us well in shillings, pounds, and pence.
Your dollars flush our regimental till,
But in more sterling coin we're richer still:
Yes, doubly, trebly, rich in your goodwill.
And so farewell! but stop, before we part,
We'll sing one song and sing it from the heart.
Just one song more: you guess the song I mean:
Our brave time-honoured hymn, 'God save the Queen.'"

He continued also to act as mentor to his younger brothers, two of whom went in due course to Cambridge, and, to his great delight, pulled in their college racing boat (Trinity Hall), which was then at the head of the river. He often visited them at Cambridge, and, whenever he could manage it, would spend some part of the vacation with them, joining them in all their amusements, and helping them in their studies. You may judge of the sort of terms they were on, by this extract from a letter to his mother in August 1856:—

"We shall be very happy to join you in Scotland. I want to know whether *good* fishing tackle is procurable at Stirling, or in the neighbourhood of Callender. At Edinbro' and Glasgow I know it can be obtained, and much cheaper than in London. Perhaps Harry can inform me, if he is not too much occupied in discovering the value of x, which I believe is the great object of mathematics (I speak it not profanely). Tell Harry and Arthur I expect to find them both without breeches.

> 'Those swelling calves were never meant
> To shun the public eye,'

as Dr. Watts remarks, or would have remarked if he had written on the subject."

Such occupations as these, with magistrate's work, and field sports taken in moderation, served to fill up his time, and would have satisfied most men situated as he was. But he could never in all these years get the notion quite out of his head (though it wore off later) that he was not doing his fair share of work in the world, and was a useless kind of personage, for whom no one was much the better but his wife and children, and whom nobody but they would miss. This feeling showed itself in his immense respect for those who were working in regular professions, and in the most conscientious scrupulousness about taking up their time. Often he has come to my chambers, and, after hurrying through some piece of family business, has insisted on going away directly, though I might not have seen him for a month, and was eager to talk on fifty subjects. The sight of open papers was enough for him; and he had not practised long enough to get the familiarity which breeds contempt, and to know how gladly the busiest lawyer puts aside an Abstract, or Interrogatories in Chancery, for the chance of a pleasant half-hour's gossip.

I think, however, that I can show you clearly enough, in a very few words, what his real work in the world was during these years, and how perfectly unconscious he was that he was doing it faithfully. In 1857, your grandfather had a dangerous attack of illness, from which he never recovered. George was with him and nursed him during the crisis. As soon as he was well enough to use a pen, he wrote as follows to Lady Salusbury :—

"Amongst other things it occurs to me how much I have had to thank God for through life, and how my family have always drawn together in the way I wished them. And here I should be doing injustice to George, if I did not in my own mind trace much of this happy result to his quiet and imperceptible influence as an elder brother, in many ways of which my wife and I were not exactly cognizant at the time. Perhaps I am thinking more about him just now as he was in his natural place as my right-hand man when I was taken unwell; and when I say truly, that neither his mother or I ever had even an unkind word or disrespectful look from him since he was born, and that his constant study through life, as far as we are concerned, has been to spare us rather than give us trouble, and throw his own personal interests over much more than we chose to allow him, it is especially for the purpose of giving dear A—— (her adopted daughter) a precedent to quote with her own lips in the training of her own boys which I know will be particularly acceptable to herself. It is the last theme on which he would like to expatiate, but that such was my deliberate and true opinion, will be, I doubt not, one of these days, a source of satisfaction to them both, and to the children."

Your grandfather died shortly afterwards, and a year later George wrote to his mother:—

"I feel that we have great cause for gratitude and rejoicing *as a family;* I mean for the way in which we hang together, and the utter absence of any subject of discord or disagreement between any of our members. I think we may well be happy, even while thinking of what happened this time last year, as I have done very frequently of late."

He would have been impatient, almost angry, if anyone had told him that the "hanging together," at which he rejoiced, was mainly his own doing.

In the village, too, he was beginning to find occupation of the most useful kind. Thus he opened a village reading-room for the labourers, which was furnished with books and papers, and lighted and warmed, every evening from seven to nine. "Hitherto it is a great success," he writes in 1868: "we have fifty members who subscribe 2*d.* a week, and we give them a cup of coffee and a biscuit for 1*d.* Some of them drink five or six cups a night. Whether coffee will continue to beat beer I don't know, but at present it keeps them from the public-house, and saves their wages for their wives. Some of them are very fond of reading, and the rest play draughts and dominoes." Then there were frequent "laundry entertainments,"—penny readings, or theatrical performances in the big laundry,—of which his sister writes: "The boys and Mr. Phillips and I used to make the music, but the great hits of the evening were always George's. He used to recite 'The One-horse Chay,' or some Ingoldsby Legend, or 'The Old Woman of Berkeley,' or sing a comic song, and the people liked his performances better than anything. Like all very reserved people, he acted wonderfully well, and always knew how every part should be done, so he used to coach us all when a play was being got up. But he would never criticise unless asked : he always thought that people knew as well as he did how to do their parts, but they did not. He was always so droll on these occasions. When a performance was proposed by the boys, he used to say it was too much trouble, and that he wanted to be left quiet. But they always got their way, and when it was inevitable he would learn his entire part while we others were mastering a page. I was always whip, because I could not stand doing anything by halves, and used to drive everyone mercilessly till the scenes began to go smoothly. He would sometimes rehearse his part almost under his breath, gabbling it off with the book in his hand, and then I would remonstrate, and he would go through it splendidly, as well as on the day of performance."

But the reform which he had most at heart he never lived to carry out. The industry of straw-plaiting, which prevails in the neighbourhood, while it enables the women and girls to earn high wages, makes them bad housewives, all their cooking and cleaning being neglected, while they run in and out of neighbours' houses, gossiping and plaiting. In the hope of curing this evil he looked forward to fitting up a large barn in the village as a sort of general meeting-place. Here, when he had made the roof air-tight, and laid down a good floor, there was to be a stove for cooking and baking, and appliances for instruction in other household work. Under his wife and sister there were to be "cooking classes, sewing classes, and singing classes; and, in the evenings, entertainments for the poor people, a piano and night classes, sometimes theatricals, and often concerts, and when the boys wanted to dance they were to have their dances there. He used to think that constant meetings in the barn would humanize us all, and be a very pleasant thing for making rich and poor meet on equal terms." It is perhaps vain to dwell upon such things, but I cannot help hoping that some day those of you who have the opportunity of realizing such plans may remember to what purposes the big barn was once destined. Of one other part of his village work, his Sunday evening classes for the big boys, I shall have to speak presently.

But you must not suppose from anything in this chapter that he ever lost his interest in politics, or public affairs. He was always a keen politician, retaining, however, all his early beliefs. "You have all got far beyond me," he writes to his sister; "and my dear mother turning Radical in her old age is delightful." Perhaps the most ardent politician amongst us all is the best witness to call on this subject. "I don't think anything was more remarkable about George than his politics. He, who was so good an old Tory in many ways, showed that he believed in a universal principle and duty underlying all the political opinions about the best means of carrying out reforms. I think it is very rare, when people are discussing politics, to find this constant recognition of something beyond party nostrums. But (as in his father) I have always detected it in George; and, when I have got very hot whilst propounding Radicalism against all the rest here, have always found sympathy from him at the bottom; and I have always felt at last how much more truly liberal he was at heart than we Radicals, because we are always wanting to force on our opinions our own way, whilst in him I always recognized a divine sort of justice and patience, which used to make me feel very conceited, and wanting in faith. He was born with aristocratic instincts, being by nature intensely sensitive and refined, with a loathing of anything blatant and in bad taste, and with an intense love of justice; and the unwise, violent, foolish way in which many men like —— expound their doctrines disgusted him beyond measure, though he would always recognize the real truth that lay at the bottom of Radicalism."

But he shall speak for himself on one great event, which you are all old enough to remember, the late war between France and Germany. Almost the first incident of the war—the despatch of the then Emperor, speaking of the Prince Imperial's "baptism of fire"—roused his indignation so strongly that it found vent in the following lines:—

> By! baby Bunting,
> Daddy's gone a hunting,
> Bath of human blood to win,
> To float his baby Bunting in.
>   By, baby Bunting.
>
> What means this hunting?
> Listen! baby Bunting—
> Wounds—that you may sleep at ease,
> Death—that you may reign in peace.
>   Sweet baby Bunting.

Yes, baby Bunting!
Jolly fun is hunting!
Jacques in front shall bleed and toil,
You in safety gorge the spoil.
    Sweet baby Bunting.

Mount! baby Bunting,
Ride to Daddy's hunting!
On its quiet cocky-horse,
Two miles in the rear, of course.
    Precious baby Bunting.

Ah, baby Bunting!
Oftentimes a hunting,
Eager riders get a spill—
Let us hope your Daddy will.
    Poor little Bunting.

Perpend, my small friend,
After all this hunting,
When the train at last moves on
Daddy's gingerbread "salon"
    May get a shunting.

Poor baby Bunting!
Curse on such a hunting!
Woe to him who bloods a child
For ambitious visions wild,
    Poor baby Bunting!

"*October 6th*, 1870.—I am, I think, rapidly changing sides about this horrid war. You know I was a tremendous Prussian at the outset, but (although the French deserve all they get) I really can't stand the bombardment of Paris; besides, Bismarck is repulsive."

"OFFLEY, 1871.

"I think that the high and mighty tone assumed by Herr Gustave Solling (German superhuman excellence, Handel, Beethoven, Minnesingers, &c.) the worst possible vehicle for the defence of the German terms of peace. When a man talks 'buncombe,' it shows that he has an uneasy feeling that his case is a weak one. The cynical line is the right one for the Germans ; why not say, in the words of Wordsworth,—

> 'And why ? Because the good old rule
> Sufficeth them ; the simple plan,
> That they should take who have the power,
> And they should keep who can.'

But pray don't say this to our cousin, and thank her for her translation. You know what I think about the matter ; I would have gone to war with the French to stop the war ; and I would have gone to war with the Germans to stop the peace. There's an Irish view of it, from a sincere war-hater."

The person who knew him best once wrote of your grandfather's politics : "Men of all parties speak of him as belonging to their clique. This proves to me, if I had required the proof to strengthen the conviction, that there is a point on the plain of politics at which the moderate Tory, the sensible Whig, and the right-minded Radical, in other words all true patriots, meet ; like the vanishing point in a picture to which all true and correct lines tend. And thus it is with him : he has reached that point, and there he foregathers with all of all parties, who, throwing aside party prejudice, act and think for the good of their fellow-creatures."

The description, I cannot but think, applied equally well to my brother, though he continued nominally a Tory to the end, and, as you will all recollect, lived as quiet, methodical a country life as if he had no interests in the world beyond crops, field sports, and petty sessions. But that it must have required a considerable effort on his part to do this comes out in much of his most intimate correspondence. For instance, only a month or two before his death he writes to his sister:—"Thanks, many, for your letter, and Mrs. S——'s. Hers is delightful, and I so fully understand her feeling. I always feel uncomfortable in point-device places, where the footman is always brushing your hat, and will insist upon putting out your clothes, and turning your socks ready to put on, and, if you say half a word, will even put them on for you. How I hate being 'valeted!' I should like to black my own boots, like Mr. ——, but then he is (or was) a master of foxhounds, and, being of course on that account a king of men, can do as he pleases, in spite of Mrs. Grundy. I am also a gypsey (is that rightly spelt? That word, and some others, are stumbling-blocks to me; I am afraid all my spelling is an affair of memory), a Bohemian at heart. I sometimes feel an almost irresistible desire to doff my breeches and paint myself blue. I should also like (I would limit myself to one month per annum) to go with a carpet-bag to the nearest station, and to rough it in all sorts of outlandish places—but then A—— can't rough it, and there are the brats, and lots of other impediments. The very act of wandering anywhere delights me. I think we spoil half the enjoyment of life by being too particular; how terrible dinner-parties are becoming! But enough of my sermon. In spite of my secret longings I shall continue to do as my neighbours, and it would be wicked in my case to be discontented. They threatened to nominate me Chairman of the Board of Guardians here, but finding that the Vice-chairman was standing (and thinking him better qualified), I declined any contest, and was not put up. I am sorry for it, for the office, although troublesome, is capable of being made useful, and I think I should have liked it in time;" and then comes a sentence which may serve to explain to some of you your feelings towards him—" I cannot forgive —— for putting ——" (one of his nephews) "on a bolting horse. If you do mount a boy, you ought to give him the cleverest and quietest horse in your stable, and no sportsman would do otherwise."

There is one more trait in his character which I must not omit here, as I wish to give you as perfect a knowledge of him as I have myself. I have already told you how very scrupulous he was with regard to money matters. He had, indeed, a horror of debt which made him morbidly sensitive on the subject; and he recognized the fact, and treated himself for it as he would have done for a fit of bile, or any other physical disorder. On more than one occasion, when some unlooked for expenditure seemed likely to bring on a more than usually severe attack, he cured himself by some piece of unwonted extravagance, such as buying a diamond ornament for his wife, or making a handsome present to some poor relation. The remedy answered perfectly in his case; but I am bound to add that it is one which I cannot recommend as a specific without the warning, that, before using it, you must satisfy yourselves, as he always did, that there were no reasonable grounds for uneasiness.

But if he sometimes worried himself about money, he kept his anxiety to himself, and was constantly doing the most liberal acts in the most thoughtful manner. Of the many instances I could give of this, I select one, which an old friend has communicated to me with permission to mention it. I give it in his own words:—
"There is one little incident connected with his personal relations to me which I shall always remember with feelings of gratitude and pleasure. When the Suez Canal was opened I had an offer of a free passage out and home in a P. and O. steamer, and I was rather exercised in my mind by not feeling it prudent to accept, as I knew that living in Egypt for a fortnight at that time would be very expensive, and I knew that I could not afford it. I happened to be writing to him about that

time, and mentioned this in my letter. By return of post he sent me a cheque for £50, begging me to accept it as a loan, to be paid when I had as much to spare, or never if I preferred it. I did not take advantage of his generous kindness, and I declare I almost regret now that I did not, as I believe I should have given him sincere pleasure in so doing."

CHAPTER X.

LETTERS TO HIS BOYS.

THE doubts as to his own usefulness in the world, noticed in the last chapter, wore off naturally as he fell into the routine of country life; but it was the growth of the younger generation—of you for whom this sketch is written—which found him in work and interest during the last years of his life. I could never have envied him anything; but if there was one talent of his more than another which I have longed to share, it was his power of winning, not only the love, but the frank confidence, of his own, and all other boys. I think the secret was, that he was far more in sympathy with them; could realize more vividly their pleasures, and troubles, than almost any man of his age. And then, he had never given up athletic games altogether, and was still a far better cricketer and football player than most boys, and ready to join them in their sports whenever they seemed to wish it.

Few things gave him more pleasure than taking up again the thread of intimate relations with his old school, which he did when his eldest nephew entered there. He accompanied him, to give him confidence and a good start, and characteristically recounts that "we had a famous football match, and I got my legs kicked to my heart's content, thereby vividly recalling old times." He remarks also, at the same time, "Rugby is charming; only there is rather too much what I call 'drill,' in the play as in the work—not spontaneous enough." Not long after, in 1866, his own eldest boy followed. He thus details that event to his mother:—

"OFFLEY, *September* 27, 1866.

"We went to Rugby last Thursday, and the new-comers were examined on Friday and Saturday. As we rather feared, Herby failed to get into the Middle School. We were rather disappointed, and he, poor boy, was in despair, as he was afraid Arnold would not take him, and that he would have to go to Mr. Furness; however, Arnold offered to make an exception in his case, and as we joyfully accepted it, Master Herby was duly installed in his uncle's study, and we left him on Monday morning very happy, and delighted with his new dignity of a public school boy. Our visit to Rugby was very pleasant, and not a little exciting. The school is much altered since my time—the boys are much more accurately dressed, less rollicking, and more decorous. The exceeding quiet of the town and playground struck me particularly. I should like to have seen a little more running about, and to have heard a little more shouting; in fact a jolly curly-haired youngster with whom I made a casual acquaintance, said to me, 'I am sure, sir, you must have had much more fun in your time than we have.' It is perhaps just as well that they should have become quieter. The recognized name for the anxious parents who bring their boys up for examination is the 'Early Fathers,' because, I suppose, they take care to be at the schoolroom-door with their Hopefuls a quarter of an hour before the examination begins. Jenny Lind's boy has just gone to the School-house; he is, as boys say, awfully 'cute, and came out nearly head of the examination. Jenny Lind was at chapel herself on Sunday; her husband has done much for the music of the school; the singing in chapel is exceedingly good, and the whole service very impressive. The last time I was in chapel there was in poor Arnold's time. The master of Herby's form, Mr. Buckoll, was my old master when I was in the shell thirty years ago! Also Mrs. Jacomb, of the principal tuck shop, used to spoil our stomachs in my time. I felt myself rather boyish again, without the boisterous spirits and good stomach of boyhood."

From this time he constantly visited the school, and kept his mother and sister informed of the progress of the boys. I add a few extracts from his letters:—

"*November*, 1866.—I was at Rugby last Saturday, and stayed over Sunday. Walter breakfasted with me on Sunday morning, and very jolly he was. He and Herby won't see much of one another until they get higher in the school. Junior boys never enter each other's boarding-houses. This is very absurd, but no power on earth can alter boys' fashions."

"EATON SOCON, *November 26th*, 1867.

"Boys' letters get so full of school slang that it is hard to understand them. Herbert says in his last that he got

100 lines from Chumley for *tweaking*. This was Hebrew to us, as 'tweaking' was not a Rugby word in my time. On referring the matter to Ned, he immediately informed us that 'tweaking' in boys' language was, shooting shot out of a catapult, or other warlike engine."

"OFFLEY, 1868.

"We have excellent accounts from Rugby. Herbert is at the head of his form, and evidently finds his work easier, and is in a high state of encouragement. One of his schoolfellows has just shot himself in the leg with a 'saloon,' meaning a saloon pistol. Hang all pistols, but boys will have them."

"OFFLEY, *October 7th*, 1868.

"Concerning schoolboys' etiquette, it beats all other etiquette. Public schools cultivate reserve, and so strongly that I think one never gets quite rid of it, although one gets better in after-life. I wish it was not so; it is one of the drawbacks of public schools, which are on the whole excellent institutions. One must take the sours with the sweets.

"Herbert would not think of speaking to a schoolfellow (not on a par with himself), unless first spoken to. And in public schools the great 'swells' are those distinguished at cricket, football, &c. Then come the sixth, by virtue of their legal power. Then the great middle class, including clever, stupid, pleasant, unpleasant, &c., and then the new boys, and the very small boys. All the power and influence is in the hands of the athletes, and the sixth form, and all the rest pay them (the athletes) the greatest respect, and the most willing obedience. They obey the sixth (lawful authority) less willingly. All this is not quite satisfactory, but it might be worse. At all events Temple, who is a tremendous Radical, knows it and allows, nay, encourages it. But I find that few people are Radicals in their own departments."

"OFFLEY, *November 7th*, 1868.

"I went for the day to see the old Rug. match, and gave Walter and Herbert a dinner at the 'Shoes' before going away. Walter played in the match, and the young ones gave it the old Rugs hot, much to my delight. Walter seemed wonderfully well, and ditto Herbert. He always looks pale at school, but he was in high spirits, and evidently enjoys school life. He is very different from me in some things; his study is awfully 'cute (that's boys' English, and means tidy and full of knick-knacks); in fact he is a bit of a dandy; I was not. Also he must be a better boy than I was, for his character is really first-rate in everything; and the masters used always to row me for not doing as much as I could. That was the burden of their song."

As a complement to these letters, I add here extracts from those to his eldest boy :—

"Thank you much for your letter received this morning; you are very good in writing so regularly, and I hope you will keep up the habit, for (I repeat) there is no pleasure to us so great as to receive your letters. We are glad to hear you are 'all right' in your form. I have no objection to the Rifle corps. It would be odd if I had, as I was a Volunteer myself; only go into it heartily, and learn your drill well. It is capital exercise, and it will do you good to be 'set up,' as you stoop too much. I should not think, however, that Temple would let the Rugby volunteers go to Windsor. If he thinks proper to do so, of course I have no objection. I suppose that as usual you are 'hard up,' so I send you a P.O. order. You must learn to exercise a little forethought and self-denial about money matters: you spend more than your income. You must overcome this habit, for it would embarrass and, perhaps, ruin you hereafter."

The next extract refers to some help in his work which his father sent him from time to time:—

"I depend upon your looking out all the words, and working it out for yourself with the help of my translation. You promised me to do this, and I know you are a boy of your word, otherwise I shouldn't think it right to help you. Your tutor may ask if you have any assistance. If he does you must say you found it very hard (which it really is for a boy of your age), and asked me to help you. There is nothing like being open and truth-telling with your masters, and every one. If he objects to my helping you, you must do the best you can without it, like a man; but I don't think he will object. Your place in the form seems very satisfactory: if you *do* get out we shall be very much pleased, but don't make yourself anxious about it, only do your best. . . . ."

Again at the beginning of the following half-year:—

"The reason you give for having lost a few places is no doubt the right one—that you have not got yet into the swing—it will be all right in a week or two. I have no doubt you will get your remove at the end of term easily enough. The *exam.* (if I understand rightly) consists of subjects which you prepare during term, and there is not much 'unseen.' This will be an advantage to you over the idle ones who don't prepare their work. I shall be delighted to help you in any way, if you will only let me know, and give me due notice. Perhaps you won't believe me when I assure you again, that Latin prose will come to you as well as cricket and football in good time; but it is the truth nevertheless. At your age I often felt the same discouragement which you feel. I had rather overgrown myself like you, and was longer 'ripening' (to use an expressive phrase) than many fellows who did not grow so fast; but it all came right in my case, as it will in yours. Therefore *en avant* and don't be discouraged. . . . ."

"We are very glad to hear that you are in upper-middle one, and it will make us very happy if you can get another remove at Christmas. It is to be done if you like, and as you cannot play football just now (worse luck) you will have more time. Don't you want some help in your tutor work? If so, send me the book; or is there anything else in which I can help you? You are now rapidly becoming a young man, and have probably some influence in the school, and will have more. Be kind to the new boys and juniors; even if they are 'scrubby,' your business is to polish them, and you will do this much better by a little kind advice than by making their lives a burden (I don't say, mind, that you are unkind to them). Don't 'bosh' your masters. Remember that they are gentlemen like yourself, and that it is insulting them to 'bosh' them when they are taking trouble with you. As to the sixth form, I don't quite approve of all the customs thereof, but it is an institution of the school, and, on the whole, beneficial, and it is no use kicking against it. Now I have done with my preaching. I don't know that it is necessary, but it can do you no harm, and I know you respect my opinion. Your mother is horrified at your signing yourself 'Hughes,' *tout court* (as the French say), so to please her don't forget to put in 'your affectionate son' (as I know you are). God bless you.

"Yours most affectionately,
"G. E. HUGHES."

"I was much pleased by your writing so openly to me. It will make me very happy if you will treat me with perfect confidence in all matters. You need have no fear that I shall not understand and sympathise with you, for although (as we have said in joke) I was a Rugbeian in the time of the ancient Britons, when we had no breeches, and painted ourselves blue for decency's sake, it seems to me a very short time since I was as you are, and I have a very vivid recollection of my youth, feelings, prejudices, faults, and all the rest of it."

And then, after some advice about his matriculation at Oxford, his father goes on:—

"I am not going to preach to you about billiards. If there had been a table at Rugby in my time (there was none), I might very possibly have played myself; although, like you, I should certainly not have made a habit of it, preferring, as I did and do, more active amusements. Don't play again at Rugby; it would be childish, as well as wrong, to risk leaving the school under a cloud, for such a paltry gratification. I don't agree with you in comparing billiards to your school games: billiards (public) generally involve smoking, and a certain amount of drinking, and losing money (or winning, which is worse); and engender a sort of lounging habit. I am afraid you have rather a fast lot at Rugby, and what you tell me about card-playing makes me rather anxious about Jack. It is altogether abominably bad form, and I wish you would get up an opposition to it. It ought to be put down for the credit of the school. I must say that there was no such card-playing in my time. Having said my say, I must leave you to do what you can, in concert with any other big fellows in the house, who may be brought to see the matter in my light."

The "Jack" referred to in the last letter was his third boy, who was now in his first term at a preparatory school for Rugby. This chapter may fitly close with his letters to this, the youngest of his boys whom he lived to see launched at school. He was a favourite subject of study to his father, who writes of him at Pau, years before: "Jack will be, I think, the strongest of the lot. He always clears his plate, fat and all, and always clears his lesson, however disagreeable;" and again, to his sister, who was the boy's godmother:—

"Your favourite Jack is always running after me, and is a very good boy, and surprisingly good company too. He has not quite forgotten how to 'beak' himself when he feels insulted. About a week ago the children had some shrimps for tea, and Jack was offended because he was presented with a 'baby' shrimp instead of a big one; so he pushed his chair from the table, and prostrated himself on his knees, with his nose in the carpet. After remaining for five minutes in that position, he felt better. It is a more amusing way of getting rid of steam than crying. Children have the funniest fancies in the world. There is a Scotch terrier next door to us, with a grave and venerable face, and a long grey beard. Jack said one day, 'that doggy like Moses coming down de mountain;' and so he really is like Moses, in one of those little woodcuts in which children delight, but I should never have thought of such a ridiculous comparison."

"Westward Ho, *October* 1871.

"Dearest Old Boy,

"Here we are all right, and I wish we had your jolly face at the other end of the table, for we miss you very much. I have begun golf, but there are not many golfers here yet; however, there is one very good player named Oliphant, so I have not much chance of the medal. Your friends the Molesworths are both gone to Radley School, near Oxford. There are only 100 boys there, but it is a nice place, and being near the Thames, they get plenty of rowing; in fact, that is their chief amusement. Ned plays golf with me, but has not got into his play yet. You are a good old boy for writing so often, and I hope you will continue it. Nothing gives us so much pleasure as your letters and Herbert's, and don't think that anything that happens to you is too trifling to tell us of. Now about your letter. I always thought that you would find the lessons rather a grind at first: you see it is your first school, and you have had no experience in working with a lot of other boys, perhaps making a row, and idling around you. Never mind. It will get easier every day, and besides, I believe that you have something of the bull-dog about you, and won't be discouraged by a little hardship and difficulty at first. I hope you will be one of your fifteen, for then I shall come up to see you play, but anyhow I am as certain as I can be of anything that you will be first-rate at football some day, and a first-rate scholar too, I hope. The two things often go together. All well, and send best love. Mamma and Argy hope your shoulder is not much hurt, and I have no doubt it is all right again. God bless you.

"Yours most affectionately,
"G. E. H.

"P.S.—I shall never think anything that you write awful bosh.'"

"OFFLEY, WESTWARD HO, 1871.

"DEAREST JACK,
"Thank you for your letters, which interest us immensely. Boys make the most absurd customs, as you will find out: it is better to give way to their customs in a good-tempered way; new boys are not admitted at once to the full privileges. It does not much matter, as I hope you won't be long at ——. Boys think it very fine and manly not to prepare their lessons, whereas in fact nothing can be more childish. Take your own way, and never mind them. It is half pretence with them, and they will respect you more if they see you have your own way. You need not stand being 'sat upon,' and yet you can be good-tempered and obliging, but, above all, don't forget what I said to you when we parted. Don't forget the lessons you have learnt at home (I don't mean Latin and Greek). God bless you. Write as often as you have time.
"Yours most affectionately,
"G. E. H."

"*October* 1871.

"DEAREST OLD BOY,
"Thank you for your letters. They are well written and spelt, and creditable to you in every way. Although it is not pleasant to us to hear that you are miserable (or rather uncomfortable, for 'miserable' is a strong word), yet we always like to hear exactly what you feel. I don't think you *can* be exactly miserable, for I believe that you are doing your best. God will not suffer us to be miserable (at least not for any time) whilst we do our duty. Don't be discouraged about your work; you see it is your first plunge into school. All your schoolfellows have had more experience than you: practice will give you the quickness and accuracy that you want.

"Your feelings towards us are quite natural: when you are at home, perfectly happy, although you do not love us less, you do not feel it so much; when you are thrown among a lot of people who do not much care about you, you find out the value of our love for you, and think more of us. However, you have Herbert, and I daresay you think that you love him better now than ever you did at home. As we are all sinful and imperfect creatures, I have no doubt that you have sometimes done and said things which we should be sorry to hear of. You must ask God to help you to do better in future; but I must say that I have always found you good and obedient, and you have never given us any anxiety. There is one lesson which you ought to learn from your present feelings of discomfort and worry; when you are a big boy at Rugby, and see any poor little fellow worried and uncomfortable, you must say a kind word to him (remembering what you once felt yourself); you have no idea how much good a kind word from a big fellow (what you call a swell) will do to a poor little beggar. You remember how kind Gardner was, and how much he was liked at Rugby for it. All are well, and send best love. I fully intend to come to see you when I get back to Offley—perhaps to the old Rug. match. God bless you.

"Yours most affectionately,
"G. E. Hughes."

"Dearest Old Boy, "*November*, 1871.

"I know why you feel rather down in the mouth just now. You have (to use a phrase in athletics) lost your first wind, and haven't yet got your *second* wind. The novelty of excitement of school life has gone off, and you are too new to it yet to enjoy what there is enjoyable in it. Courage! I know your feelings well, having experienced them myself. So has Herbert: so, in short, has everyone who has ever been at school. You will soon get over it all, and like your school life, although of course it is not so pleasant as home. Most schoolboys are selfish and bad-mannered, and there are always plenty of snobs and bullies amongst them; but there is always a minority of nice fellows. I am inclined to believe that as you go so often to Arnold's, you have not made much acquaintance with your schoolfellows. Perhaps it would be better to cultivate their acquaintance more. Don't be afraid about not getting into Rugby. You ought to have heard Herbert's doleful forebodings about never being able to get out of lower school: he was much more doleful than you, but if you were to remind him of it, he would probably not remember it at all; neither will you a year hence. If you are hungry, can't you buy grub in the town? I mean something like sausage-rolls, or hard eggs. I will give you the money for it; or can you suggest any way in which we can supply you? What do you do on Sundays? and to what church do you go? I wish we could have you with us occasionally, just as much as you do. All are well, and join in best love. God bless you.

"Yours most affectionately,

"G. E. Hughes."

"Dearest Old Boy, "Offley.

"I believe your mamma has written to you, but I must give you a few lines to say how much we were pleased with your report which came this morning. There is no happiness in this world so great to us as the assurance that you and your brothers are doing well. I am very sorry that you were down in the mouth at my departure. I should like to have you always with me, but you (being a boy of good sense) must know very well that it cannot be: you must (like all others) fly from the nest some time or other, and school is the preparation for a longer flight. I have no doubt that now you are all right again. You won't be downhearted long, if you only work well and do your duty. At your age the spirits are very elastic, and soon recover any depression.

"We shall be anxious to hear about your cough and Sharp's opinion. God bless you,

"Yours most affectionately,
"G. E. H."

"OFFLEY, *Sunday, Nov.* 26*th*, 1871.

"DEAREST OLD BOY,

"I have nothing particular to tell you, but must write a line in return for your jolly letters, which are very pleasant to us. I am very sorry that your cough is not better. I am afraid that you will not get rid of it until we get you at home, and nurse you properly. You will soon be with us now; in the meantime take care of yourself, and make the most of your time (I don't think I need tell you to work, as you seem so well inclined already). I will write about your coming home, and also about your going up for the entrance Exam. after Christmas. I wish very much that you should go up. I really don't see why you should go to Rugby three days before the Exam.; but if they insist upon it, I suppose it must be so. I hope you won your match yesterday. It is very unfortunate that you could not play as you would have done but for this unlucky cough. Never mind, you have plenty of time before you for football. All are well, and join in best love to you. God bless you.

"Yours most affectionately,
"G. E. HUGHES.

"The hounds come to Wellbury to-morrow. I hope your game was good. Let us know."

At the beginning of the next term Jack went to Rugby, and almost the first letter he received from his father was the following Valentine, which species of missive appears to have become popular amongst boys:—

"*February* 23, 1872.

"This is the month when little Cu-
 -pid robs us of our senses, oh!
'Tis he inspires me to renew
My doleful strains of love to you,
Oh, charming, fascinating cru-
 -el Walter Jacky Mansfield Hugh-
 -es, Scholæ Rugbeiensis, oh!

"I learn to dance and sew, while you
 Are learning Latin tenses, oh!
How I should like to dance with *you*,
Instead of with my frightful grew-
 -some governess, oh! charming cru-
 -el Walter Jacky Mansfield Hugh-
 -es, Scholæ Rugbeiensis, oh!

"I'm sure the least that you can do
 To calm my nerves and senses, oh!
Is (though 'tis slightly overdue)
To take this little billet-doux,
And be the Valentine so true
Of her who signs herself your Su-
 -san, charming, fascinating cru-
 -el Walter Jacky Mansfield Hugh-
 -es, Scholæ Rugbeiensis, oh!
   " YOUR SUSAN."

In explanation of an allusion in the next letter, I insert an extract of the same date, from one to his sister:—

"Jack is in high force, but has been having extra lessons (with all his schoolfellows), in consequence of (what he calls) a 'towel fight,' and subsequent 'war dance,' in which the school indulged in an irrepressible burst of youthful spirits. What geese boys are!"

"OFFLEY, *March* 1872.

"DEAREST JACK,

"I hope you got the hamper all right, and that the 'grub' was good and of the right sort. Your 'war dance' amused us excessively, and of course there is no harm in a war dance; but, if it is forbidden, what an old goose you are to risk having impositions and extra lessons for it! But schoolboys are always the same, and I can't expect you to be wiser than the rest.

"If you can't make out why your copies are wrong, why don't you ask one of your schoolfellows? I suppose some of them are good fellows, and would tell you your mistake; or say openly to the master that you can't find out, and I should think he would enlighten you. At least, he *ought*. We shall have you home in about three weeks, and right glad we shall be. Go at it hard for the remainder of the term, for remember the entrance Exam. You must work a little in the holidays to keep up what you know. The boys are better, and have been playing football vigorously. Best love to Herbert; ask him whether he wants any cricket practice. I mean Hughes to bowl. God bless you.

"Yours most affectionately,
"G. E. H."

Westward Ho, from which several of the preceding letters were written, had become his favourite watering-place. He had gone there at first by chance, and, finding links and a golf club, had taken to the game with his usual success. At Pau he had played a little, but certainly never handled a club till he was past forty. Nevertheless, though it is a game in which, I am told, early training and constant practice is almost an essential condition of success, he entered for, and succeeded in winning the champion's medal in the annual gathering of 1870. Soon after his return from the meeting he wrote to me.

"We spent three very pleasant weeks at Westward Ho. I wish that I could infect you with 'golfomania.' Golf is *the* middle-aged man's game. I mean by the middle-aged man, the man who could *once*, but cannot *now*, get down upon a leg shooter. We had a dozen hard-worked men from the city, besides doctors, lawyers, soldiers on leave, etc., all perfectly mad whilst it lasted. I was quite as mad as the rest, and having now 'relapsed' into sanity, I am able to look back upon it with the most intense amusement. The humour of the whole thing was positively sublime. You have heard squires at their wine after a good run—bless you, they can't hold a candle to golfers. Most of the players were Scotch, and the earnestness with which the Scotch 'play' is a caution. I think of trying my hand at a rhapsody about golf."

The rhapsody was, I believe, never written, but he continued to like and practise the game till his death, which indeed is, in my mind, rather painfully connected with it. My last visit to Offley was in the short Easter vacation of this year, and I thought I had never seen him better, or in more full vigour of body and mind. On the 30th of March he mounted me, and I rode with him and two of his boys to a meet near Offley. We had a run early in the day, and got home to a late lunch, after which he went out into his plantations and worked till dark. Indeed, when I left the same evening by the mail train for the north, I beguiled my journey by thinking that the whole kingdom might be searched in vain to find a finer specimen of a man. On that day four weeks I received a telegram from Hoylake to say that he was lying there very dangerously ill. He had gone on there, after leaving his boys at Rugby, to take part in the golf tournament. He went down with a bad cold, but paid no attention to it, and went round the links with some friends on the first evening. The next day he became much worse, and was obliged to take to his bed, from which he never got up. The cold had settled on his lungs, and violent inflammation was set up. His wife and children were summoned at once, and his mother and sister and myself two days later. When I arrived, the lower part of the lungs had suppurated, and the medical man gave very slight hopes of his recovery. He could only speak with exceeding difficulty, but retained his strength, and the grip of his hand was as strong as ever. He met death with the same courage as he had shown throughout life, giving me a few clear instructions for a codicil to his will, while his youngest boy lay with his head on his shoulder, crying bitterly, and almost with his last breath regretting the trouble he was giving his nurse. On the afternoon of May 1st he received the Sacrament with all of us, and at four on the morning of the 2nd passed away, leaving behind him, I am proud to think, no braver or better man. But you shall have better testimony than mine on this point. Out of the many letters to the same purpose which I received, and two of which have found a place in the earlier part of this memoir, I select an extract from one written by Bishop MacDougal, who, thirty years ago, had rowed behind him in the University boat.

"I must just write a line to express my heartfelt sympathy with you in your sad, sad bereavement. Dear old George! What an irreparable loss to you and all his old friends! I have myself been heavy-hearted ever since I heard he had been called away from us, and shall never think of his cheery voice, his hearty greeting, his kindly, loving words, without a sharp pang of regret that I shall no more in this life meet with him I loved so well, and admired as the finest specimen of the high-minded, earnest, true-hearted English gentleman it has been my lot to meet with. He was too good for this hard, selfish generation, and he is in God's mercy called away to that better world, where love and truth and peace dwell undisturbed in the presence of our blessed Lord. May we, my dear Tom, have grace given us so to fight the good fight of truth and faith, that when our work is done we may be called thither to join your dear brother and our other loved ones, who have gained the victory over self and the world, and have been called to their rest before us."

CHAPTER XI.

CONCLUSION.

On looking through the preceding pages, I have been struck with one special shortcoming. I am painfully conscious how poor and shallow the picture here attempted will be, in any case, to those who knew my brother best. Nevertheless, those for whom it was undertaken will, I trust, be able to get from it some clearer idea of the outer life of their father and uncle, but of that which underlies the outer life they will learn almost nothing. And yet how utterly inadequate must be any knowledge of a human being which does not get beneath this surface! How difficult to do so to any good purpose! For that "inner," or "eternal," or "religious" life (call it which you will, they all mean the same thing) is so entirely a matter between each human soul and God, is at best so feebly and imperfectly expressed by the outer life. But, difficult as it may be, the attempt must be made; for I find that I cannot finish my task with a good conscience without making it.

There is not one of you, however young, but must be living two lives—and the sooner you come to recognize the fact clearly, the better for you—the one life in the outward material world, in contact with the things which you can see, and taste, and handle, which are always changing and passing away: the other in the invisible, in contact with the unseen; with that which does not change or pass away—which is the same yesterday, to-day, and for ever. The former life you must share with others, with your family, your schoolfellows and friends, with everyone you meet in business or pleasure. The latter you must live alone, in the solitude of your own inmost being, if you can find no Spirit there communing with yours—in the presence of, and in communion with, the Father of your spirit, if you are willing to recognize that presence. The one life will no doubt always be the visible expression of the other; just as the body is the garment in which the real man is clothed for his sojourn in time. But the expression is often little more than a shadow, unsatisfying, misleading. One of our greatest English poets has written—

> "The one remains, the many change and pass,
>   Heaven's light for ever shines, earth's shadows fly.
> Time, like a dome of many coloured glass,
>   Stains the bright radiance of eternity,
>   Until death tramples it to fragments."

And so you and I are living now under the dome of many-coloured glass, and shall live as long as we remain in these bodies, a temporal and an eternal life—"the next world," which too many of our teachers speak of as a place which we shall first enter after death, being in fact "next" only in the truest sense of the word; namely, that it is "nearest" to us now. The dome of time can do nothing more (if we even allow it to do that) than partially to conceal from us the light which is always there, beneath, around, above us.

"The outer life of the devout man," it has been well said, "should be thoroughly attractive to others. He would be simple, honest, straightforward, unpretending, gentle, kindly;—his conversation cheerful and sensible; he would be ready to share in all blameless mirth, indulgent to all save sin." And tried by this test, the best we have at command, my brother was essentially a devout man.

The last thirty years, the years of his manhood, have been a period of great restlessness and activity, chiefly of a superficial kind, in matters pertaining specially to religion. The Established Church, of which he was a member, from conviction as well as by inheritance, has been passing through a crisis which has often threatened her existence; faction after faction, as they saw their chance, rising up and striving in the hope of casting out those whose opinions or practices they disliked. Against all such attempts my brother always protested whenever he had an opportunity, and discouraged all those with whom he had any influence from taking any part in them.

"I have no patience," for instance, he writes at one of these crises, "with —— for mixing himself up with Church politics. I believe you know what I think about them, namely, that both parties are right in some things and wrong in others, and that the truth lies between the two. I hope I shall always be able to express my dissent from both without calling names or imputing motives, and when I hear others doing so, I am always inclined, like yourself, to defend the absent. I was very sorry to hear that —— has given up his parish. I cannot understand his excessive attachment to what is, after all, only the outside of religion; but he is so good a man, so hard-working, so self-denying, that one feels what a great loss he must be."

Outside the Church the same religious unrest has had several noteworthy results, perhaps the most remarkable of these being a negative one: I mean, the aggressive attitude and movement of what is popularly known as scientific thought. Amongst its leaders have been, and are, some of the best, as well as the ablest, men of our time, who have had, as they deserved to have, a very striking influence. But the tone of scientific men towards religion has been uniformly impatient or contemptuous, not seldom petulant. "Why go on troubling yourselves and mankind about that of which you can know nothing?" they have said. "This 'eternal' or 'inner' life of which you prate is wholly beyond your ken. We can prove to you that much of your so-called theology rests on unsound premises. Be content to work and learn with us in the material world, of which alone you can get to know anything certain." That challenge has shaken the foundations of much which called itself faith in our day. I never could discover that my brother was ever seriously troubled by it. Dissertations on the Mosaic cosmogony, theories of the origin of species, speculations on the antiquity of man, and the like, interested, but never seemed to rouse in him any of the alarm or anger which they have excited in so many good Christians. Granting all that they tend to prove, they deal only with the outward garment, with the visible universe, and the life which must be lived in it, leaving the inner and real life of mankind quite untouched.

He was, however, neither so tolerant of, nor I think so fair to, the stirring of thought within the Church, which has resulted in criticisms supposed to be destructive of much that was held sacred in the last generation. His keen sense of loyalty was offended by anything which looked like an attack coming from within the ranks, and so he shared the feeling so widely, and I think wrongly, entertained by English Churchmen, that the right of free thought and free speech on the most sacred subjects should be incompatible with holding office in the Church.

As to his own convictions on such subjects, he was extremely reserved, owing to a tendency which he believed he had detected in himself to religious melancholy, which he treated simply as a disease. But no one who knew him at all could ever doubt that a genuine and deep religious faith was the basis of his character, and those who knew him best testify unanimously to its ever increasing power. "I don't know if you were ever told," his sister writes, "of the singular desire dying people had that George should be with them. You know how reserved he was, and he would always think that people would prefer some one who talked more to them, but I think it was his great gentleness and strength which made the dying feel him such a comfort. He never volunteered; but when sent for, as was often the case, always went to them, and read and prayed constantly with them as long as they lived. There was one poor young man who died of consumption, and George was constantly with him to the last. The father was a very disreputable character, and George seldom saw him. But some time after the young man's death, the father met George in the fields, and threw himself on his knees to bless him for his love for his dead son. George came home much shocked that the man should have knelt to him. One old man, whom he used to go to for weeks and weeks during his long last illness, really adored him, and, when George was away for a short time, prayed that he might live till he saw him again. And George was back before he died."

Of this old man, he writes himself to his mother:—

"My old friend died on Saturday morning. I mean Tom Pearse, for fifty years an honest labourer in this parish. I am very sorry that (as he died in the short hours) I could not be with him at the last, but very glad that he died before I left Offley. So was he. He prayed every day to die, not that he suffered, but he had such a strong faith that death would be much better. He said to me almost the last time I saw him, 'I thought, sir, I should have been home before this.' And when he was taken worse at last, he asked the nurse, 'Am I going home?' 'Yes.' 'I'm so glad,' he answered, and died soon after. What an euthanasia! All good people call death going home. 'Let me die the death of the righteous, and my last end be like his.'"

Intercourse of the most sacred and intimate kind with the old, and dying, and suffering of another station in life is, however, far easier to a man of reserved temper than it is with the young and healthy. The most difficult class to reach in country villages, as in our great towns, is that which is entering life, not that which is thinking of quitting it. You may get young men together for cricket or football, or even for readings, or in a club, and attain in the process a certain familiarity with them, useful enough in its way, but not approaching the kind of intimacy which should exist between people passing their lives in the same small community. The effort to do anything more with a class just emancipated from control, full of strength and health, and as a rule suspicious of advances from those in a rank above their own, must always be an exceedingly difficult one to make for such a man as my brother, and is rarely successful. He made it, and succeeded. During all the winter months, on every Sunday evening the young men and the elder boys of the village were invited to his house, and quite a number of them used to come regularly. They were received by him and his wife. First he would read a passage of Scripture, and explain and comment on it, and afterwards he or his wife read to them some amusing book. He used to speak with the greatest delight of the pleasure which these meetings seemed to give, and of their excellent effect on his own relations with the young men and boys who frequented them. When the time for separating came, they used all to say the Apostles' Creed, the Lord's Prayer, and the following short prayer which he wrote[1] for the purpose:—

"O Lord God, Thou knowest all things. Thou seest us by night as well as by day. We pray Thee, for Christ's sake, forgive us whatever we have done wrong this day. May we be sorry for our sins, and believe in Jesus Christ, who died for sinners. May the Holy Spirit make us holy. Take care of us this night, whilst we are asleep. Bless our fathers and mothers, brothers and sisters, and all our relations and friends, and do them good, for Christ's sake. Help us to be good as long as we live, and when we die, may we go to heaven and be happy for ever, because Christ died for us. Amen."

If I were to write a volume, I could throw no clearer light on the inner life of my brother than shines out of

[1] Since this was printed I have heard that the prayer was not written by him, but only adapted for the use of the boys from a collection of some Church Society.

this short simple prayer, written for village boys, and repeated with them week by week. Nor is there any other picture of him that I would rather leave on your minds than this. When I think of the help and strength which he has been to me and many more, the noble lines on All Saints' Day, of the poet I have already quoted in this memoir, seem to be haunting me, and with them I will end.

> "Such lived not in the past alone,
>   But thread to-day the unheeding street,
> And stairs to sin and sorrow known
>   Sing to the welcome of their feet.
>
> "The den they enter glows a shrine,
>   The grimy sash an oriel burns,
> Their cup of water warms like wine,
>   Their speech is filled from heavenly urns.
>
> "Around their brows to me appears
>   An aureole traced in tenderest light,
> The rainbow gleam of smiles thro' tears,
>   In dying eyes by them made bright,
>
> "Of souls who shivered on the edge
>   Of that chill ford, repassed no more,
> And in their mercy felt the pledge
>   And sweetness of the farther shore."

FINIS.

BEDFORD STREET, COVENT GARDEN, LONDON.
November, 1872.

MACMILLAN & CO.'S CATALOGUE of Works in BELLES LETTRES, including Poetry, Fiction, Works on Art, Critical and Literary Essays, etc.

Allingham.—LAURENCE BLOOMFIELD IN IRELAND; or, the New Landlord. By WILLIAM ALLINGHAM. New and Cheaper Issue, with a Preface. Fcap. 8vo. cloth. 4s. 6d.

The aim of this little book is to do something, however small, towards making Ireland, yet so little known to the general British public, better understood. Several of the most important problems of life, Irish life and human life, are dealt with in their principles, according to the author's best lights. In the new Preface, the state of Ireland, with special reference to the Church measure, is discussed. "It is vital with the national character. . . . . It has something of Pope's point and Goldsmith's simplicity, touched to a more modern issue."—ATHENÆUM.

Archer.—CHRISTINA NORTH. By E. M. ARCHER. Two vols. Crown 8vo. 21s.

"The work of a clever cultivated person, wielding a practised pen. The characters are drawn with force and precision, the dialogue is easy: the whole book displays powers of pathos and humour, and a shrewd knowledge of men and things."—SPECTATOR.

Arnold.—Works by MATTHEW ARNOLD :—

THE COMPLETE POETICAL WORKS. Vol. I. NARRATIVE AND ELEGIAC POEMS. Vol. II. DRAMATIC AND LYRIC POEMS. Extra fcap. 8vo. Price 6s. each.

Arnold—*continued.*

The two volumes comprehend the First and Second Series of the Poems, and the New Poems. "*Thyrsis is a poem of perfect delight, exquisite in grave tenderness of reminiscence, rich in breadth of western light, breathing full the spirit of gray and ancient Oxford.*"—SATURDAY REVIEW. "*The noblest in it is clothed in clearest words. There is no obscurity, no useless ornament: everything is simple, finished, and perfect.*"—SCOTSMAN.

ESSAYS IN CRITICISM. New Edition, with Additions. Extra fcap. 8vo. 6s.

The Essays in this Volume are—"The Function of Criticism at the Present Time;" "The Literary Influence of Academies;" "Maurice de Guerin;" "Eugenie de Guerin;" "Heinrich Heine;" "Pagan and Mediæval;" "Religious Sentiment;" "Joubert;" "Spinoza and the Bible;" "Marcus Aurelius." Both from the subjects dealt with and mode of treatment, few books are more calculated to delight, inform, and stimulate than these charming Essays.

Baker.—(For other Works by the same Author, see CATALOGUE OF TRAVELS.)

CAST UP BY THE SEA; OR, THE ADVENTURES OF NED GREY. By SIR SAMUEL BAKER, M.A., F.R.G.S. With Illustrations by HUARD. Fourth Edition. Crown 8vo. cloth gilt. 7s. 6d.

"*An admirable tale of adventure, of marvellous incidents, wild exploits, and terrible dénouements.*"—DAILY NEWS. "*A story of adventure by sea and land in the good old style.*"—PALL MALL GAZETTE.

Baring-Gould.—Works by S. BARING-GOULD, M.A. :—

IN EXITU ISRAEL. An Historical Novel. Two Vols. 8vo. 21s.

"*Some of its most powerful passages — and prodigiously powerful they are—are descriptions of familiar events in the earlier days of the Revolution.*"—LITERARY CHURCHMAN. "*Full of the*

Baring-Gould—*continued.*

> *most exciting incidents and ably portrayed characters, abounding in beautifully attractive legends, and relieved by descriptions fresh, vivid, and truth-like."*—WESTMINSTER REVIEW.

LEGENDS OF OLD TESTAMENT CHARACTERS, from the Talmud and other sources. Two vols. Crown 8vo. 16s. Vol. I. Adam to Abraham. Vol. II. Melchizedek to Zachariah.

> *Mr. Baring-Gould has here collected from the Talmud and other sources, Jewish and Mohammedan, a large number of curious and interesting legends concerning the principal characters of the Old Testament, comparing these frequently with similar legends current among many of the nations, savage and civilized, all over the world.* "*These volumes contain much that is very strange, and, to the ordinary English reader, very novel."*—DAILY NEWS.

Barker.—Works by LADY BARKER :—

> "*Lady Barker is an unrivalled story-teller."*—GUARDIAN.

STATION LIFE IN NEW ZEALAND. New and Cheaper Edition. Crown 8vo. 3s. 6d.

> *These letters are the exact account of a lady's experience of the brighter and less practical side of colonization. They record the expeditions, adventures, and emergencies diversifying the daily life of the wife of a New Zealand sheep-farmer; and, as each was written while the novelty and excitement of the scenes it describes were fresh upon her, they may succeed in giving here in England an adequate impression of the delight and freedom of an existence so far removed from our own highly-wrought civilization.* "*We have never read a more truthful or a pleasanter little book."*—ATHENÆUM.

SPRING COMEDIES. STORIES.

CONTENTS :—A Wedding Story—A Stupid Story—A Scotch Story—A Man's Story. Crown 8vo. 7s. 6d.

> "*Lady Barker is endowed with a rare and delicate gift for narrating stories,—she has the faculty of throwing even into her printed narrative a soft and pleasant tone, which goes far to make the reader think the subject or the matter immaterial, so long as the author will go on telling stories for his benefit."*—ATHENÆUM.

Barker—*continued.*

STORIES ABOUT :—With Six Illustrations. Third Edition. Extra fcap. 8vo. 4s. 6d.

This volume contains several entertaining stories about Monkeys, Jamaica, Camp Life, Dogs, Boys, &c. "There is not a tale in the book which can fail to please children as well as their elders." —PALL MALL GAZETTE.

A CHRISTMAS CAKE IN FOUR QUARTERS. With Illustrations by JELLICOE. Third Edition. Extra fcap. 8vo. cloth gilt. 4s. 6d.

In this little volume, Lady Barker, whose reputation as a delightful story-teller is established, narrates four pleasant stories showing how the "Great Birth-day" is kept in the "Four Quarters" of the globe,—in England, Jamaica, India, and New Zealand. The volume is illustrated by a number of well-executed cuts. "Contains just the stories that children should be told. 'Christmas Cake' is a delightful Christmas book."—GLOBE.

RIBBON STORIES. With Illustrations by C. O. MURRAY. Extra fcap. 8vo. cloth gilt. 4s. 6d.

Bell.—ROMANCES AND MINOR POEMS. By HENRY GLASSFORD BELL. Fcap. 8vo. 6s.

"Full of life and genius."—COURT CIRCULAR.

Besant.—STUDIES IN EARLY FRENCH POETRY. By WALTER BESANT, M.A. Crown. 8vo. 8s. 6d.

A sort of impression rests on most minds that French literature begins with the "siècle de Louis Quatorze;" any previous literature being for the most part unknown or ignored. Few know anything of the enormous literary activity that began in the thirteenth century, was carried on by Rulebeuf, Marie de France, Gaston de Foix, Thibault de Champagne, and Lorris; was fostered by Charles of Orleans, by Margaret of Valois, by Francis the First; that gave a crowd of versifiers to France, enriched, strengthened, developed, and fixed the French language, and prepared the way for Corneille and for Racine. The present work aims to afford information and direction touching the early efforts of France in poetical literature. "In one moderately sized volume he has contrived to introduce us to the very best, if not to all of the early French poets."—ATHENÆUM.

Black (W).—THE STRANGE ADVENTURES OF A PHAETON. By W. BLACK, Author of "A Daughter of Heth." Second Edition. Two vols. Crown 8vo. 21s.

Brimley.—ESSAYS BY THE LATE GEORGE BRIMLEY, M.A. Edited by the Rev. W. G. CLARK, M.A. With Portrait. Cheaper Edition. Fcap. 8vo. 2s. 6d.

George Brimley was regarded by those who knew him as "one of the finest critics of the day." The Essays contained in this volume are all more or less critical, and were contributed by the author to some of the leading periodicals of the day. The subjects are, " Tennyson's Poems," " Wordsworth's Poems," " Poetry and Criticism," " The Angel in the House," Carlyle's "Life of Sterling," "Esmond," " My Novel," "Bleak House," " Westward Ho!" Wilson's "Noctes Ambrosianæ," Comte's " Positive Philosophy." "It will," JOHN BULL *says, " be a satisfaction to the admirers of sound criticism and unassuming common sense to find that the Essays of the late George Brimley have reappeared in a new and popular form. They will give a healthy stimulus to that spirit of inquiry into the real value of our literary men whose names we too often revere without sufficient investigation."*

Broome.—THE STRANGER OF SERIPHOS. A Dramatic Poem. By FREDERICK NAPIER BROOME. Fcap. 8vo. 5s.

Founded on the Greek legend of Danaë and Perseus. "Grace and beauty of expression are Mr. Broome's characteristics; and these qualities are displayed in many passages."—ATHENÆUM. *" The story is rendered with consummate beauty."*—LITERARY CHURCHMAN.

Burke.—EDMUND BURKE, a Historical Study. By JOHN MORLEY, B.A., Oxon. Crown 8vo. 7s. 6d.

" The style is terse and incisive, and brilliant with epigram and point. Its sustained power of reasoning, its wide sweep of observation and reflection, its elevated ethical and social tone, stamp it as

a work of high excellence."—SATURDAY REVIEW. "A model of compact condensation. We have seldom met with a book in which so much matter was compressed into so limited a space."—PALL MALL GAZETTE. "An essay of unusual effort."—WESTMINSTER REVIEW.

Carroll.—Works by "LEWIS CARROLL:"—

ALICE'S ADVENTURES IN WONDERLAND. With Forty-two Illustrations by TENNIEL. 36th Thousand. Crown 8vo. cloth. 6s.

A GERMAN TRANSLATION OF THE SAME. With TENNIEL'S Illustrations. Crown 8vo. gilt. 6s.

A FRENCH TRANSLATION OF THE SAME. With TENNIEL'S Illustrations. Crown 8vo. gilt. 6s.

AN ITALIAN TRANSLATION OF THE SAME. By T. P. ROSSETTE. With TENNIEL'S Illustrations. Crown 8vo. 6s.

"*Beyond question supreme among modern books for children.*"— SPECTATOR. "*One of the choicest and most charming books ever composed for a child's reading.*"—PALL MALL GAZETTE. "*A very pretty and highly original book, sure to delight the little world of wondering minds, and which may well please those who have unfortunately passed the years of wondering.*"—TIMES.

THROUGH THE LOOKING-GLASS, AND WHAT ALICE FOUND THERE. With Fifty Illustrations by TENNIEL. Crown 8vo. 6s. 28th Thousand.

In the present volume is described, with inimitably clever and laughter-moving nonsense, the further Adventures of the fairy-favoured Alice, in the grotesque world which she found to exist on the other side of her mother's drawing-room looking-glass, through which she managed to make her way. The work is profusely embellished with illustrations by Tenniel, exhibiting as great an amount of humour as those to which "Alice's Adventures in Wonderland" owed so much of its popularity.

Chatterton: A BIOGRAPHICAL STUDY. By DANIEL WILSON, LL.D., Professor of History and English Literature in University College, Toronto. Crown 8vo. 6s. 6d.

The author here regards Chatterton as a Poet, not as a "mere resetter and defacer of stolen literary treasures." Reviewed in this light, he has found much in the old materials capable of being turned to new account: and to these materials research in various directions has enabled him to make some additions. He believes that the boy-poet has been misjudged, and that the biographies hitherto written of him are not only imperfect but untrue. While dealing tenderly, the author has sought to deal truthfully with the failings as well as the virtues of the boy: bearing always in remembrance, what has been too frequently lost sight of, that he was but a boy;—a boy, and yet a poet of rare power. The EXAMINER *thinks this "the most complete and the purest biography of the poet which has yet appeared."*

Church (A. J.)—HORÆ TENNYSONIANÆ, Sive Eclogæ e Tennysono Latine redditæ. Cura A. J. CHURCH, A.M. Extra fcap. 8vo. 6s.

Latin versions of Selections from Tennyson. Among the authors are the Editor, the late Professor Conington, Professor Seeley, Dr. Hessey, Mr. Kebbel, and other gentlemen. "Of Mr. Church's ode we may speak in almost unqualified praise, and the same may be said of the contributions generally."—PALL MALL GAZETTE.

Clough (Arthur Hugh).—THE POEMS AND PROSE REMAINS OF ARTHUR HUGH CLOUGH. With a Selection from his Letters and a Memoir. Edited by his Wife. With Portrait. Two Vols. Crown 8vo. 21s.

The late Professor Clough is well known as a graceful, tender poet, and as the scholarly translator of Plutarch. The letters possess high interest, not biographical only, but literary—discussing, as they do, the most important questions of the time, always in a genial spirit. The "Remains" include papers on "Retrenchment at Oxford;" on Professor F. W. Newman's book, "The Soul;" on Wordsworth; on the Formation of Classical English; on some Modern Poems (Matthew Arnold and the late Alexander Smith), &c. &c. "Taken as a whole," the SPECTATOR *says, "these volumes cannot fail to be a lasting monument of one of the most original men of our age." "Full of charming letters from Rome," says the* MORNING STAR, *"from Greece, from America, from Oxford, and from Rugby."*

Clough (Arthur Hugh)—*continued.*

THE POEMS OF ARTHUR HUGH CLOUGH, sometime Fellow of Oriel College, Oxford. Third Edition. Fcap. 8vo. 6*s.*

  "*From the higher mind of cultivated, all-questioning, but still conservative England, in this our puzzled generation, we do not know of any utterance in literature so characteristic as the poems of Arthur Hugh Clough.*"—FRASER'S MAGAZINE.

Clunes.—THE STORY OF PAULINE: an Autobiography. By G. C. CLUNES. Crown 8vo. 6*s.*

  "*Both for vivid delineation of character and fluent lucidity of style, 'The Story of Pauline' is in the first rank of modern fiction.*"—GLOBE. "*Told with delightful vivacity, thorough appreciation of life, and a complete knowledge of character.*"—MANCHESTER EXAMINER.

Collects of the Church of England. With a beautifully Coloured Floral Design to each Collect, and Illuminated Cover. Crown 8vo. 12*s.* Also kept in various styles of morocco.

  In this richly embellished edition of the Church Collects, the paper is thick and handsome and the type large and beautiful, each Collect, with a few exceptions, being printed on a separate page. The distinctive characteristic of this edition is the floral design which accompanies each Collect, and which is generally emblematical of the character of the day or saint to which it is assigned; the flowers which have been selected are such as are likely to be in bloom on the day to which the Collect belongs. Each flower is richly but tastefully and naturally printed in colours, and from the variety of plants selected and the faithfulness of the illustrations to nature, the volume should form an instructive and interesting companion to all devout Christians, who are likely to find their devotions assisted and guided by having thus brought before them the flowers in their seasons, God's beautiful and never-failing gifts to men. The Preface explains the allusion in the case of all those illustrations which are intended to be emblematical of the days to which they belong, and the Table of Contents forms a complete botanical index, giving both the popular and scientific name of each plant. There are at least one hundred separate plants figured. "*This is beyond question,*" *the* ART JOURNAL *says,* "*the most beautiful book of the season.*"

"*Carefully, indeed livingly drawn and daintily coloured,*" *says the* PALL MALL GAZETTE. *The* GUARDIAN *thinks it* "*a successful attempt to associate in a natural and unforced manner the flowers of our fields and gardens with the course of the Christian year.*"

Cox.—RECOLLECTIONS OF OXFORD. By G. V. COX, M.A., late Esquire Bedel and Coroner in the University of Oxford. Second and cheaper Edition. Crown 8vo. 6s.

Mr. Cox's Recollections date from the end of last century to quite recent times. They are full of old stories and traditions, epigrams and personal traits of the distinguished men who have been at Oxford during that period. The TIMES *says that it "will pleasantly recall in many a country parsonage the memory of youthful days."*

Dante.—DANTE'S COMEDY, THE HELL. Translated by W. M. ROSSETTI. Fcap. 8vo. cloth. 5s.

"*The aim of this translation of Dante may be summed up in one word—Literality. To follow Dante sentence for sentence, line for line, word for word—neither more nor less, has been my strenuous endeavour.*"—AUTHOR'S PREFACE.

Days of Old; STORIES FROM OLD ENGLISH HISTORY. By the Author of "Ruth and her Friends." New Edition. 18mo. cloth, gilt leaves. 3s. 6d.

The Contents of this interesting and instructive volume are, "*Caradoc and Deva,*" *a story of British life in the first century;* "*Wolfgan and the Earl; or, Power,*" *a story of Saxon England: and* "*Roland,*" *a story of the Crusaders.* "*Full of truthful and charming historic pictures, is everywhere vital with moral and religious principles, and is written with a brightness of description, and with a dramatic force in the representation of character, that have made, and will always make, it one of the greatest favourites with reading boys.*"—NONCONFORMIST.

Deane.—MARJORY. By MILLY DEANE. Second Edition. Crown 8vo. 4s. 6d.

The TIMES *of September* 11*th says it is* "*A very touching story, full of promise for the after career of the authoress. It is so tenderly* drawn, and so full of life and grace, that any attempt to analyse or describe it falls sadly short of the original. We will venture to say that few readers of any natural feeling or sensibility will take up 'Marjory' without reading it through at a sitting, and we hope we shall see more stories by the same hand." The MORNING POST calls it "*A deliciously fresh and charming little love story.*"

De Vere.—THE INFANT BRIDAL, and other Poems. By AUBREY DE VERE. Fcap. 8vo. 7s. 6d.

"*Mr. De Vere has taken his place among the poets of the day. Pure and tender feeling, and that polished restraint of style which is called classical, are the charms of the volume.*"—SPECTATOR.

Doyle (Sir F. H.)—Works by Sir FRANCIS HASTINGS DOYLE, Professor of Poetry in the University of Oxford:—

THE RETURN OF THE GUARDS, AND OTHER POEMS. Fcap. 8vo. 7s.

"*Good wine needs no bush, nor good verse a preface; and Sir Francis Doyle's verses run bright and clear, and smack of a classic vintage. . . . His chief characteristic, as it is his greatest charm, is the simple manliness which gives force to all he writes. It is a characteristic in these days rare enough.*"—EXAMINER.

LECTURES ON POETRY, delivered before the University of Oxford in 1868. Crown 8vo. 3s. 6d.

THREE LECTURES:—(1) *Inaugural, in which the nature of Poetry is discussed;* (2) *Provincial Poetry;* (3) *Dr. Newman's "Dream of Gerontius."* "*Full of thoughtful discrimination and fine insight: the lecture on 'Provincial Poetry' seems to us singularly true, eloquent, and instructive.*"—SPECTATOR. "*All these dissertations are marked by a scholarly spirit, delicate taste, and the discriminating powers of a trained judgment.*"—DAILY NEWS.

Dürer, Albrecht.—HISTORY OF THE LIFE OF ALBRECHT DÜRER, of Nürnberg. With a Translation of his Letters and Journal, and some account of his Works. By Mrs. CHARLES HEATON. Royal 8vo. bevelled boards, extra gilt. 31s. 6d.

This work contains about Thirty Illustrations, ten of which are productions by the autotype (carbon) process, and are printed in permanent tints by Messrs. Cundall and Fleming, under licence from the Autotype Company, Limited; the rest are Photographs and Woodcuts.

Estelle Russell.—By the Author of "The Private Life of Galileo." Crown 8vo. 6s.

Full of bright pictures of French life. The English family, whose fortunes form the main drift of the story, reside mostly in France, but there are also many English characters and scenes of great interest. It is certainly the work of a fresh, vigorous, and most interesting writer, with a dash of sarcastic humour which is refreshing and not too bitter. "We can send our readers to it with confidence."—SPECTATOR.

Evans.—BROTHER FABIAN'S MANUSCRIPT, AND OTHER POEMS. By SEBASTIAN EVANS. Fcap. 8vo. cloth. 6s.

"*In this volume we have full assurance that he has 'the vision and the faculty divine.' . . . Clever and full of kindly humour.*"—GLOBE.

Fairy Book.—The Best Popular Fairy Stories. Selected and Rendered anew by the Author of "John Halifax, Gentleman." With Coloured Illustrations and Ornamental Borders by J. E. ROGERS, Author of "Ridicula Rediviva." Crown 8vo. cloth, extra gilt. 6s. (Golden Treasury Edition. 18mo. 4s. 6d.)

"*A delightful selection, in a delightful external form.*"—SPECTATOR. *Here are reproduced in a new and charming dress many old favourites, as "Hop-o'-my-Thumb," "Cinderella," "Beauty and the Beast," "Jack the Giant-killer," "Tom Thumb," "Rumpelstilzchen," "Jack and the Bean-stalk," "Red Riding-Hood," "The Six Swans," and a great many others. "A book which will prove delightful to children all the year round."*—PALL MALL GAZETTE.

Fletcher.—THOUGHTS FROM A GIRL'S LIFE. By LUCY FLETCHER. Second Edition. Fcap. 8vo. 4s. 6d.

"*Sweet and earnest verses, especially addressed to girls, by one who can sympathise with them, and who has endeavoured to give articulate utterance to the vague aspirations after a better life of pious endeavour, which accompany the unfolding consciousness of the inner life in girlhood. The poems are all graceful; they are marked throughout by an accent of reality; the thoughts and emotions are genuine.*"—ATHENÆUM.

Freeman (E. A., Hon. D.C.L.) — HISTORICAL ESSAYS. By EDWARD FREEMAN, M.A., Hon. D.C.L., late Fellow of Trinity College, Oxford. Second Edition. 8vo. 10s. 6d.

This volume contains twelve Essays selected from the author's contributions to various Reviews. The principle on which they were chosen was that of selecting papers which referred to comparatively modern times, or, at least, to the existing states and nations of Europe. By a sort of accident a number of the pieces chosen have thrown themselves into something like a continuous series bearing on the historical causes of the great events of 1870—71. *Notes have been added whenever they seemed to be called for; and whenever he could gain in accuracy of statement or in force or clearness of expression, the author has freely changed, added to, or left out, what he originally wrote. To many of the Essays has been added a short note of the circumstances under which they were written. It is needless to say that any product of Mr. Freeman's pen is worthy of attentive perusal; and it is believed that the contents of this volume will throw light on several subjects of great historical importance and the widest interest. The following is a list of the subjects:*—I. "The Mythical and Romantic Elements in Early English History;" II. "The Continuity of English History;" III. "The Relations between the Crowns of England and Scotland;" IV. "St. Thomas of Canterbury and his Biographers;" V. "The Reign of Edward the Third;" VI. "The Holy Roman Empire;" VII. "The Franks and the Gauls;" VIII. "The Early Sieges of Paris;" IX. "Frederick the First, King of Italy;" X. "The Emperor Frederick the Second;" XI. "Charles the Bold;" XII. "Presidential Government."—"*All of them are well worth reading, and very agreeable to read. He never touches a question without adding to our comprehension of it, without leaving the impression of an ample knowledge, a righteous purpose, a clear and powerful understanding.*"—SATURDAY REVIEW.

Freeman (E. A., Hon. D.C.L.)—*continued.*
A SECOND SERIES OF HISTORICAL ESSAYS.
In the Press.

Garnett.—IDYLLS AND EPIGRAMS. Chiefly from the Greek Anthology. By RICHARD GARNETT. Fcap. 8vo. 2s. 6d.

"*A charming little book. For English readers, Mr. Garnett's translations will open a new world of thought.*"—WESTMINSTER REVIEW.

Geikie.—SCENERY OF SCOTLAND, viewed in Connexion with its Physical Geology. By ARCHIBALD GEIKIE, F.R.S., Director of the Geological Survey of Scotland. With Illustrations and a New Geological Map. Crown 8vo. 10s. 6d.

"*Before long, we doubt not, it will be one of the travelling companions of every cultivated tourist in Scotland.*"—EDINBURGH COURANT. "*Amusing, picturesque, and instructive.*"—TIMES. "*There is probably no one who has so thoroughly mastered the geology of Scotland as Mr. Geikie.*"—PALL MALL GAZETTE.

Gladstone.—JUVENTUS MUNDI. The Gods and Men of the Heroic Age. By the Right Hon. W. E. GLADSTONE, M.P. Crown 8vo. cloth extra. With Map. 10s. 6d. Second Edition.

"*This new work of Mr. Gladstone deals especially with the historic element in Homer, expounding that element and furnishing by its aid a full account of the Homeric men and the Homeric religion. It starts, after the introductory chapter, with a discussion of the several races then existing in Hellas, including the influence of the Phœnicians and Egyptians. It contains chapters "On the Olympian System, with its several Deities;" "On the Ethics and the Polity of the Heroic Age;" "On the Geography of Homer;" "On the Characters of the Poems;" presenting, in fine, a view of primitive life and primitive society as found in the poems of Homer. To this New Edition various additions have been made. "To read these brilliant details," says the* ATHENÆUM, "*is like standing on the Olympian threshold and gazing at the ineffable brightness within." According to the* WESTMINSTER REVIEW, "*it would be difficult to point out a book that contains so much fulness of knowledge along with so much freshness of perception and clearness of presentation.*"

Guesses at Truth.—By Two Brothers. With Vignette Title, and Frontispiece. New Edition, with Memoir. Fcap. 8vo. 6s. Also see Golden Treasury Series.

> *These "Guesses at Truth" are not intended to tell the reader what to think. They are rather meant to serve the purpose of a quarry in which, if one is building up his opinions for himself, and only wants to be provided with materials, he may meet with many things to suit him. To very many, since its publication, has this work proved a stimulus to earnest thought and noble action; and thus, to no small extent, it is believed, has it influenced the general current of thinking during the last forty years. It is now no secret that the authors were* AUGUSTUS *and* JULIUS CHARLES HARE. *"They—living as they did in constant and free interchange of thought on questions of philosophy and literature and art; delighting, each of them, in the epigrammatic terseness which is the charm of the 'Pensées' of Pascal, and the 'Caractères' of La Bruyère—agreed to utter themselves in this form, and the book appeared, anonymously, in two volumes, in* 1827."

Hamerton.—Works by PHILIP GILBERT HAMERTON :—

A PAINTER'S CAMP. Second Edition, revised. Extra fcap. 8vo. 6s.

BOOK I. *In England;* BOOK II. *In Scotland;* BOOK III. *In France.*

> *This is the story of an Artist's encampments and adventures. The headings of a few chapters may serve to convey a notion of the character of the book: A Walk on the Lancashire Moors; the Author his own Housekeeper and Cook; Tents and Boats for the Highlands; The Author encamps on an uninhabited Island; A Lake Voyage; A Gipsy Journey to Glencoe; Concerning Moonlight and Old Castles; A little French City; A Farm in the Autunois, &c. &c. "These pages, written with infinite spirit and humour, bring into close rooms, back upon tired heads, the breezy airs of Lancashire moors and Highland lochs, with a freshness which no recent novelist has succeeded in preserving."*—NONCONFORMIST. *"His pages sparkle with many turns of expression, not a few well-told anecdotes, and many observations which are the fruit of attentive study and wise reflection on the complicated phenomena of human life, as well as of unconscious nature."*—WESTMINSTER REVIEW.

Hamerton—*continued.*

ETCHING AND ETCHERS. A Treatise Critical and Practical. With Original Plates by REMBRANDT. CALLOT, DUJARDIN, PAUL POTTER, &c. Royal 8vo. Half morocco. 31s. 6d.

"*The work is one which deserves to be consulted by every intelligent admirer of the fine arts, whether he is an etcher or not.*"— GUARDIAN.

"*It is not often we get anything like the combined intellectual and æsthetic treat which is supplied us by Mr. Hamerton's ably written and handsome volume. It is a work of which author, printer, and publisher may alike feel proud. It is a work, too, of which none but a genuine artist could by possibility have been the author.*"— SATURDAY REVIEW.

Hervey.—DUKE ERNEST, a Tragedy; and other Poems. Fcap. 8vo. 6s.

"*Conceived in pure taste and true historic feeling, and presented with much dramatic force. . . . . Thoroughly original.*"—BRITISH QUARTERLY.

Higginson.—MALBONE: An Oldport Romance. By T. W. HIGGINSON. Fcap. 8vo. 2s. 6d.

This is a story of American life, so told as to be interesting and instructive to all English readers. The DAILY NEWS says: "Who likes a quiet story, full of mature thought, of clear humorous surprises, of artistic studious design? 'Malbone' is a rare work, possessing these characteristics, and replete, too, with honest literary effort."

Hillside Rhymes.—Extra fcap. 8vo. 5s.

Home.—BLANCHE LISLE, and other Poems. By CECIL HOME. Fcap. 8vo. 4s. 6d.

Hood (Tom).—THE PLEASANT TALE OF PUSS AND ROBIN AND THEIR FRIENDS, KITTY AND BOB. Told in Pictures by L. FRÖLICH, and in Rhymes by TOM HOOD. Crown 8vo. gilt. 3s. 6d.

This is a pleasant little tale of wee Bob and his Sister, and their attempts to rescue poor Robin from the cruel claws of Pussy. It will be intelligible and interesting to the meanest capacity, and is illustrated by thirteen graphic cuts drawn by Frölich. "The volume is prettily got up, and is sure to be a favourite in the nursery." —SCOTSMAN. *"Herr Frölich has outdone himself in his pictures of this dramatic chase."*—MORNING POST.

Jebb.—THE CHARACTERS OF THEOPHRASTUS. An English Translation from a Revised Text. With Introduction and Notes. By R. C. JEBB, M.A., Fellow and Assistant Tutor of Trinity College, Cambridge, and Public Orator of the University. Extra fcap. 8vo. 6s. 6d.

The first object of this book is to make these lively pictures of old Greek manners better known to English readers. But as the Editor and Translator has been at considerable pains to procure a reliable text, and has recorded the results of his critical labours in a lengthy Introduction, in Notes and Appendices, it is hoped that the work will prove of value even to the scholar. "We must not omit to give due honour to Mr. Jebb's translation, which is as good as translation can be. . . . Not less commendable are the execution of the Notes and the critical handling of the text."—SPECTATOR. *"Mr. Jebb's little volume is more easily taken up than laid down."*—GUARDIAN.

Keary (A.)—Works by Miss A. KEARY :—

JANET'S HOME. Cheap Edition. Globe 8vo. 2s. 6d.

"Never did a more charming family appear upon the canvas; and most skilfully and felicitously have their characters been portrayed. Each individual of the fireside is a finished portrait, distinct and lifelike. . . . The future before her as a novelist is that of becoming the Miss Austin of her generation."—SUN.

CLEMENCY FRANKLYN. Globe 8vo. 2s. 6d.

"Full of wisdom and goodness, simple, truthful, and artistic. . . It is capital as a story; better still in its pure tone and wholesome influence."—GLOBE.

OLDBURY. Three vols. Crown 8vo. 31s. 6d.

"This is a very powerfully written story."—GLOBE. *"This is a*

really excellent novel."—ILLUSTRATED LONDON NEWS. *" The sketches of society in Oldbury are excellent. The pictures of child life are full of truth."*—WESTMINSTER REVIEW.

Keary (A. and E.)—Works by A. and E. KEARY:—

THE LITTLE WANDERLIN, and other Fairy Tales. 18mo. 3s. 6d.

" The tales are fanciful and well written, and they are sure to win favour amongst little readers."—ATHENÆUM.

THE HEROES OF ASGARD. Tales from Scandinavian Mythology. New and Revised Edition, illustrated by HUARD. Extra fcap. 8vo. 4s. 6d.

" Told in a light and amusing style, which, in its drollery and quaintness, reminds us of our old favourite Grimm."—TIMES.

Kingsley.—Works by the Rev. CHARLES KINGSLEY, M.A., Rector of Eversley, and Canon of Chester:—

Canon Kingsley's novels, most will admit, have not only commanded for themselves a foremost place in literature, as artistic productions of a high class, but have exercised upon the age an incalculable influence in the direction of the highest Christian manliness. Mr. Kingsley has done more perhaps than almost any other writer of fiction to fashion the generation into whose hands the destinies of the world are now being committed. His works will therefore be read by all who wish to have their hearts cheered and their souls stirred to noble endeavour; they must *be read by all who wish to know the influences which moulded the men of this century.*

"WESTWARD HO!" or, The Voyages and Adventures of Sir Amyas Leigh. Sixth Edition. Crown 8vo. 6s.

No other work conveys a more vivid idea of the surging, adventurous, nobly inquisitive spirit of the generations which immediately followed the Reformation in England. The daring deeds of the Elizabethan heroes are told with a freshness, an enthusiasm, and a truthfulness that can belong only to one who wishes he had been their leader. His descriptions of the luxuriant scenery of the then new-found Western land are acknowledged to be unmatched. FRASER'S MAGAZINE *calls it " almost the best historical novel of the day."*

Kingsley (C.)—*continued.*

TWO YEARS AGO. Fourth Edition. Crown 8vo. 6s.

"*Mr. Kingsley has provided us all along with such pleasant diversions—such rich and brightly tinted glimpses of natural history, such suggestive remarks on mankind, society, and all sorts of topics, that amidst the pleasure of the way, the circuit to be made will be by most forgotten.*"—GUARDIAN.

HYPATIA; or, New Foes with an Old Face. Fifth Edition. Crown 8vo. 6s.

The work is from beginning to end a series of fascinating pictures of strange phases of that strange primitive society; and no finer portrait has yet been given of the noble-minded lady who was faithful to martyrdom in her attachment to the classical creeds. No work affords a clearer notion of the many interesting problems which agitated the minds of men in those days, and which, in various phases, are again coming up for discussion at the present time.

HEREWARD THE WAKE—LAST OF THE ENGLISH. Crown 8vo. 6s.

Mr. Kingsley here tells the story of the final conflict of the two races, Saxons and Normans, as if he himself had borne a part in it. While as a work of fiction "Hereward" cannot fail to delight all readers, no better supplement to the dry history of the time could be put into the hands of the young, containing as it does so vivid a picture of the social and political life of the period.

YEAST: A Problem. Fifth Edition. Crown 8vo. 5s.

In this production the author shows, in an interesting dramatic form, the state of fermentation in which the minds of many earnest men are with regard to some of the most important religious and social problems of the day.

ALTON LOCKE. New Edition. With a New Preface. Crown 8vo. 4s. 6d.

This novel, which shows forth the evils arising from modern "caste," has done much to remove the unnatural barriers which existed between the various classes of society, and to establish a sympathy to

Kingsley (C.)—*continued.*

some extent between the higher and lower grades of the social scale. Though written with a purpose, it is full of character and interest; the author shows, to quote the SPECTATOR, "*what it is that constitutes the true Christian, God-fearing, man-living gentleman.*"

AT LAST: A CHRISTMAS IN THE WEST INDIES. With numerous Illustrations. Second and Cheaper Edition. Crown 8vo. 10s. 6d.

Mr. Kingsley's dream of forty years was at last *fulfilled, when he started on a Christmas expedition to the West Indies, for the purpose of becoming personally acquainted with the scenes which he has so vividly described in* "*Westward ho!*" "*In this book Mr. Kingsley revels in the gorgeous wealth of West Indian vegetation, bringing before us one marvel after another, alternately sating and piquing our curiosity. Whether we climb the cliffs with him, or peer over into narrow bays which are being hollowed out by the trade-surf, or wander through impenetrable forests, where the tops of the trees form a green cloud overhead, or gaze down glens which are watered by the clearest brooks, running through masses of palm and banana and all the rich variety of foliage, we are equally delighted and amazed.*"—ATHENÆUM.

THE WATER BABIES. A Fairy Tale for a Land Baby. New Edition, with additional Illustrations by Sir NOEL PATON, R.S.A., and P. SKELTON. Crown 8vo. cloth extra gilt. 5s.

"*In fun, in humour, and in innocent imagination, as a child's book we do not know its equal.*"—LONDON REVIEW. "*Mr. Kingsley must have the credit of revealing to us a new order of life. . . . There is in the 'Water Babies' an abundance of wit, fun, good humour, geniality, élan, go.*"—TIMES.

THE HEROES; or, Greek Fairy Tales for my Children. With Coloured Illustrations. New Edition. 18mo. 4s. 6d.

"*We do not think these heroic stories have ever been more attractively told. . . There is a deep under-current of religious feeling traceable throughout its pages which is sure to influence young readers powerfully.*"—LONDON REVIEW. "*One of the children's books that will surely become a classic.*"—NONCONFORMIST.

Kingsley (C.)—*continued.*

PHAETHON; or, Loose Thoughts for Loose Thinkers. Third Edition. Crown 8vo. 2s.

> "*The dialogue of 'Phaethon' has striking beauties, and its suggestions may meet half-way many a latent doubt, and, like a light breeze, lift from the soul clouds that are gathering heavily, and threatening to settle down in misty gloom on the summer of many a fair and promising young life.*"—SPECTATOR.

POEMS; including The Saint's Tragedy, Andromeda, Songs, Ballads, etc. Complete Collected Edition. Extra fcap. 8vo. 6s.

> *Canon Kingsley's poetical works have gained for their author, independently of his other works, a high and enduring place in literature, and are much sought after. The publishers have here collected the whole of them in a moderately-priced and handy volume. The* SPECTATOR *calls "Andromeda" "the finest piece of English hexameter verse that has ever been written. It is a volume which many readers will be glad to possess."*

Kingsley (H.)—Works by HENRY KINGSLEY:—

TALES OF OLD TRAVEL. Re-narrated. With Eight full-page Illustrations by HUARD. Fourth Edition. Crown 8vo. cloth, extra gilt. 5s.

> *In this volume Mr. Henry Kingsley re-narrates, at the same time preserving much of the quaintness of the original, some of the most fascinating tales of travel contained in the collections of Hakluyt and others. The* CONTENTS *are:—Marco Polo; The Shipwreck of Pelsart; The Wonderful Adventures of Andrew Battel; The Wanderings of a Capuchin; Peter Carder; The Preservation of the "Terra Nova;" Spitzbergen; D'Ermenonville's Acclimatization Adventure; The Old Slave Trade; Miles Philips; The Sufferings of Robert Everard; John Fox; Alvaro Nunez; The Foundation of an Empire. "We know no better book for those who want knowledge or seek to refresh it. As for the 'sensational,' most novels are tame compared with these narratives."*—ATHENÆUM. "*Exactly the book to interest and to do good to intelligent and high-spirited boys.*"—LITERARY CHURCHMAN.

Kingsley (H.)—*continued.*

THE LOST CHILD. With Eight Illustrations by FRÖLICH. Crown 4to. cloth gilt. 3s. 6d.

> *This is an interesting story of a little boy, the son of an Australian shepherd and his wife, who lost himself in the bush, and who was, after much searching, found dead far up a mountain-side. It contains many illustrations from the well-known pencil of Frölich.* "*A pathetic story, and told so as to give children an interest in Australian ways and scenery.*"—GLOBE. "*Very charmingly and very touchingly told.*"—SATURDAY REVIEW.

Knatchbull-Hugessen.—Works by E. H. KNATCHBULL-HUGESSEN, M.P. :—

> *Mr. Knatchbull-Hugessen has won for himself a reputation as an inimitable teller of fairy-tales.* "*His powers,*" *says the* TIMES, "*are of a very high order; light and brilliant narrative flows from his pen, and is fed by an invention as graceful as it is inexhaustible.*" "*Children reading his stories,*" *the* SCOTSMAN *says,* "*or hearing them read, will have their minds refreshed and invigorated as much as their bodies would be by abundance of fresh air and exercise.*"

STORIES FOR MY CHILDREN. With Illustrations. Fourth Edition. Extra fcap. 8vo. 5s.

> "*The stories are charming, and full of life and fun.*"—STANDARD. "*The author has an imagination as fanciful as Grimm himself, while some of his stories are superior to anything that Hans Christian Andersen has written.*"—NONCONFORMIST.

CRACKERS FOR CHRISTMAS. More Stories. With Illustrations by JELLICOE and ELWES. Fifth Edition. Crown 8vo. 5s.

> "*A fascinating little volume, which will make him friends in every household in which there are children.*"—DAILY NEWS.

MOONSHINE: Fairy Tales. With Illustrations by W. BRUNTON. Fifth Edition. Crown 8vo. cloth gilt. 5s.

> *Here will be found* "*an Ogre, a Dwarf, a Wizard, quantities of Elves and Fairies, and several animals who speak like mortal men and women.*" *There are twelve stories and nine irresistible illustrations.*

Knatchbull-Hugessen—*continued.*

> "*A volume of fairy tales, written not only for ungrown children, but for bigger, and if you are nearly worn out, or sick, or sorry, you will find it good reading.*"—GRAPHIC. "*The most charming volume of fairy tales which we have ever read. . . . We cannot quit this very pleasant book without a word of praise to its illustrator. Mr. Brunton from first to last has done admirably.*"—TIMES.

TALES AT TEA-TIME. Fairy Stories. With Seven Illustrations by W. BRUNTON. Crown 8vo. cloth gilt. 5s.

Knatchbull-Hugessen (Louisa).—THE HISTORY OF PRINCE PERRYPETS. A Fairy Tale. By LOUISA KNATCHBULL-HUGESSEN. With Eight Illustrations by WEIGAND. Crown 4to. cloth gilt. 3s. 6d.

Latham.—SERTUM SHAKSPERIANUM, Subnexis aliquot aliunde excerptis floribus. Latine reddidit Rev. H. LATHAM, M.A. Extra fcap. 8vo. 5s.

> *Besides versions of Shakespeare, this volume contains, among other pieces, Gray's "Elegy," Campbell's "Hohenlinden," Wolfe's "Burial of Sir John Moore," and selections from Cowper and George Herbert.*

Lemon.—THE LEGENDS OF NUMBER NIP. By MARK LEMON. With Illustrations by C. KEENE. New Edition. Extra fcap. 8vo. 2s. 6d.

Life and Times of Conrad the Squirrel. A Story for Children. By the Author of "Wandering Willie," "Effie's Friends," &c. With a Frontispiece by R. FARREN. Second Edition. Crown 8vo. 3s. 6d.

> *It is sufficient to commend this story of a Squirrel to the attention of readers, that it is by the author of the beautiful stories of "Wandering Willie" and "Effie's Friends." It is well calculated to make children take an intelligent and tender interest in the lower animals.*

Little Estella, and other Fairy Tales for the Young. Royal 16mo. 3s. 6d.

> "This is a fine story, and we thank heaven for not being too wise to enjoy it."—DAILY NEWS.

Lowell.—AMONG MY BOOKS. Six Essays. By J. R. LOWELL. Dryden—Witchcraft—Shakespeare once More—New England Two Centuries Ago—Lessing—Rousseau and the Sentimentalists. Crown 8vo. 7s. 6d.

> "We may safely say the volume is one of which our chief complaint must be that there is not more of it. There are good sense and lively feeling forcibly and tersely expressed in every page of his writing."—PALL MALL GAZETTE.

COMPLETE POETICAL WORKS of JAMES RUSSELL LOWELL. With Portrait. One vol. 18mo.

Lyttelton.—Works by LORD LYTTELTON :—

THE "COMUS" OF MILTON, rendered into Greek Verse. Extra fcap. 8vo. 5s.

THE "SAMSON AGONISTES" OF MILTON, rendered into Verse. Extra fcap. 8vo. 6s. 6d.

> "Classical in spirit, full of force, and true to the original."—GUARDIAN.

Macmillan's Magazine.—Published Monthly. Price 1s. Volumes I. to XXVI. are now ready. 7s. 6d. each.

Macquoid.—PATTY. By KATHERINE S. MACQUOID. Two vols. Crown 8vo. 21s.

> The ATHENÆUM "congratulates Mrs. Macquoid on having made a great step since the publication of her last novel," and says this "is a graceful and eminently readable story." The GLOBE considers it "well-written, amusing, and interesting, and has the merit of being out of the ordinary run of novels."

Marlitt (E.)—THE COUNTESS GISELA. Translated from the German of E. MARLITT. Crown 8vo. 7s. 6d.

> "A very beautiful story of German country life."—LITERARY CHURCHMAN.

Masson (Professor).—Works by DAVID MASSON, M.A., Professor of Rhetoric and English Literature in the University of Edinburgh. (See also BIOGRAPHICAL and PHILOSOPHICAL CATALOGUES.)

BRITISH NOVELISTS AND THEIR STYLES. Being a Critical Sketch of the History of British Prose Fiction. Crown 8vo. 7s. 6d.

"*Valuable for its lucid analysis of fundamental principles, its breadth of view, and sustained animation of style.*"—SPECTATOR. "*Mr. Masson sets before us with a bewitching ease and clearness which nothing but a perfect mastery of his subject could have rendered possible, a large body of both deep and sound discriminative criticism on all the most memorable of our British novelists. . . . . His brilliant and instructive book.*"—JOHN BULL.

Mazini.—IN THE GOLDEN SHELL; A Story of Palermo. By LINDA MAZINI. With Illustrations. Globe 8vo. cloth gilt. 4s. 6d.

Merivale.—KEATS' HYPERION, rendered into Latin Verse. By C. MERIVALE, B.D. Second Edition. Extra fcap. 8vo. 3s. 6d.

Milner.—THE LILY OF LUMLEY. By EDITH MILNER. Crown 8vo. 7s. 6d.

"*The novel is a good one and decidedly worth the reading.*"— EXAMINER. "*A pretty, brightly-written story.*"—LITERARY CHURCHMAN. "*A tale possessing the deepest interest.*"—COURT JOURNAL.

Mistral (F.)—MIRELLE, a Pastoral Epic of Provence. Translated by H. CRICHTON. Extra fcap. 8vo. 6s.

"*It would be hard to overpraise the sweetness and pleasing freshness of this charming epic.*"—ATHENÆUM. "*A good translation of a poem that deserves to be known by all students of literature and friends of old-world simplicity in story-telling.*"—NONCONFORMIST.

MR. PISISTRATUS BROWN, M.P., IN THE HIGHLANDS. New and Cheap Issue. Crown 8vo. 2s. 6d.

"*The book is calculated to recall pleasant memories of holidays well spent, and scenes not easily to be forgotten. To those who have never been in the Western Highlands, or sailed along the Frith of Clyde and on the Western Coast, it will seem almost like a fairy story. There is a charm in the volume which makes it anything but easy for a reader who has opened it to put it down until the last page has been read.*"—SCOTSMAN.

Mrs. Jerningham's Journal. A Poem purporting to be the Journal of a newly-married Lady. Second Edition. Fcap. 8vo. 3s. 6d.

"*It is nearly a perfect gem. We have had nothing so good for a long time, and those who neglect to read it are neglecting one of the jewels of contemporary history.*"—EDINBURGH DAILY REVIEW. "*One quality in the piece, sufficient of itself to claim a moment's attention, is that it is unique—original, indeed, is not too strong a word—in the manner of its conception and execution.*" —PALL MALL GAZETTE.

Mitford (A. B.)—TALES OF OLD JAPAN. By A. B. MITFORD, Second Secretary to the British Legation in Japan. With Illustrations drawn and cut on Wood by Japanese Artists. Two Vols. Crown 8vo. 21s.

The old Japanese civilization is fast disappearing, and will, in a few years, be completely extinct. It was important, therefore, to preserve as far as possible trustworthy records of a state of society which, although venerable from its antiquity, has for Europeans the charm of novelty; hence the series of narratives and legends translated by Mr. Mitford, and in which the Japanese are very judiciously left to tell their own tale. The two volumes comprise not only stories and episodes illustrative of Asiatic superstitions, but also three sermons. The Preface, Appendices, and Notes explain a number of local peculiarities; the thirty-one woodcuts are the genuine work of a native artist, who, unconsciously of course, has adopted the process first introduced by the early German masters. "They will always be interesting as memorials of a most exceptional society; while, regarded simply as tales, they are sparkling, sensational, and dramatic, and the originality of their ideas and the quaintness of their language give them a most captivating piquancy.

The illustrations are extremely interesting, and for the curious in such matters have a special and particular value."—PALL MALL GAZETTE.

Myers (Ernest).—THE PURITANS. By ERNEST MYERS. Extra fcap. 8vo. cloth. 2s. 6d.

"It is not too much to call it a really grand poem, stately and dignified, and showing not only a high poetic mind, but also great power over poetic expression."—LITERARY CHURCHMAN.

Myers (F. W. H.)—POEMS. By F. W. H. MYERS. Containing "St. Paul," "St. John," and others. Extra fcap. 8vo. 4s. 6d.

"It is rare to find a writer who combines to such an extent the faculty of communicating feelings with the faculty of euphonious expression."—SPECTATOR. *"'St. Paul' stands without a rival as the noblest religious poem which has been written in an age which beyond any other has been prolific in this class of poetry. The sublimest conceptions are expressed in language which, for richness, taste, and purity, we have never seen excelled."*—JOHN BULL.

Nine Years Old.—By the Author of "St. Olave's," "When I was a Little Girl," &c. Illustrated by FRÖLICH. Third Edition. Extra fcap. 8vo. cloth gilt. 4s. 6d.

It is believed that this story, by the favourably known author of "St. Olave's," will be found both highly interesting and instructive to the young. The volume contains eight graphic illustrations by Mr. L. Frölich. The EXAMINER says: *"Whether the readers are nine years old, or twice, or seven times as old, they must enjoy this pretty volume."*

Noel.—BEATRICE, AND OTHER POEMS. By the Hon. RODEN NOEL. Fcap. 8vo. 6s.

"It is impossible to read the poem through without being powerfully moved. There are passages in it which for intensity and tenderness, clear and vivid vision, spontaneous and delicate sympathy, may be compared with the best efforts of our best living writers."—SPECTATOR. *"It is long since we have seen a volume of poems which has seemed to us so full of the real stuff of which we are made, and uttering so freely the deepest wants of this complicated age."*—BRITISH QUARTERLY.

Norton.—Works by the Hon. Mrs. NORTON :—

THE LADY OF LA GARAYE. With Vignette and Frontispiece. New Edition. Fcap. 8vo. 4s. 6d.

"*A poem entirely unaffected, perfectly original, so true and yet so fanciful, so strong and yet so womanly, with painting so exquisite, a pure portraiture of the highest affections and the deeepest sorrows, and instilling a lesson true, simple, and sublime.*" — DUBLIN UNIVERSITY MAGAZINE. "*Full of thought well expressed, and may be classed among her best efforts.*"—TIMES.

OLD SIR DOUGLAS. Cheap Edition. Globe 8vo. 2s. 6d.

"*This varied and lively novel—this clever novel so full of character, and of fine incidental remark.*"— SCOTSMAN. "*One of the pleasantest and healthiest stories of modern fiction.*"—GLOBE.

Oliphant.—Works by Mrs. OLIPHANT :—

AGNES HOPETOUN'S SCHOOLS AND HOLIDAYS. New Edition with Illustrations. Royal 16mo. gilt leaves. 4s. 6d.

"*There are few books of late years more fitted to touch the heart, purify the feeling, and quicken and sustain right principles.*"— NONCONFORMIST. "*A more gracefully written story it is impossible to desire.*"—DAILY NEWS.

A SON OF THE SOIL. New Edition. Globe 8vo. 2s. 6d.

"*It is a very different work from the ordinary run of novels. The whole life of a man is portrayed in it, worked out with subtlety and insight.*"—ATHENÆUM. "*With entire freedom from any sensational plot, there is enough of incident to give keen interest to the narrative, and make us feel as we read it that we have been spending a few hours with friends who will make our own lives better by their own noble purposes and holy living.*"—BRITISH QUARTERLY REVIEW.

Our Year. A Child's Book, in Prose and Verse. By the Author of "John Halifax, Gentleman." Illustrated by CLARENCE DOBELL. Royal 16mo. 3s. 6d.

"*It is just the book we could wish to see in the hands of every child.*" —ENGLISH CHURCHMAN.

Olrig Grange. Edited by HERMANN KUNST, Philol. Professor. Extra fcap. 8vo. 6s. 6d.

> This is a poem in six parts, each the utterance of a distinct person. It is the story of a young Scotchman of noble aims designed for the ministry, but who "rent the Creed trying to fit it on," who goes to London to seek fame and fortune in literature, and who returns defeated to his old home in the north to die. The NORTH BRITISH DAILY MAIL, in reviewing the work, speaks of it as affording "abounding evidence of genial and generative faculty working in self-decreed modes. A masterly and original power of impression, pouring itself forth in clear, sweet, strong rhythm. . . . Easy to cull, remarkable instances of thrilling fervour, of glowing delicacy, of scathing and trenchant scorn, to point out the fine and firm discrimination of character which prevails throughout, to dwell upon the ethical power and psychological truth which are exhibited, to note the skill with which the diverse parts of the poem are set in organic relation. . . . It is a fine poem, full of life, of music, and of clear vision."

Oxford Spectator, the. — Reprinted. Extra fcap. 8vo. 3s. 6d.

> These papers, after the manner of Addison's "Spectator," appeared in Oxford from November 1867 to December 1868, at intervals varying from two days to a week. They attempt to sketch several features of Oxford life from an undergraduate's point of view, and to give modern readings of books which undergraduates study. "There is," the SATURDAY REVIEW says, "all the old fun, the old sense of social ease and brightness and freedom, the old medley of work and indolence, of jest and earnest, that made Oxford life so picturesque."

Palgrave (W. Gifford).—ESSAYS ON EASTERN QUESTIONS. By W. GIFFORD PALGRAVE. 8vo. 10s. 6d.

CONTENTS :—Mahometanism in the Levant—The Mahometan Revival—The Turkomans and other Tribes of the North-East Turkish Frontier—Eastern Christians—The Monastery of Sumelas—The Abkhasian Insurrection—The Poet Omar—The Brigand Ta' Abbet Shurran.

Palgrave.—Works by FRANCIS TURNER PALGRAVE, M.A., late Fellow of Exeter College, Oxford :—

ESSAYS ON ART. Extra fcap. 8vo. 6s.

Mulready—Dyce—Holman Hunt—Herbert—Poetry, Prose, and Sensationalism in Art—Sculpture in England—The Albert Cross, &c. Most of these Essays have appeared in the SATURDAY REVIEW *and elsewhere: but they have been minutely revised, and in some cases almost re-written, with the aim mainly of excluding matters of temporary interest, and softening down all asperities of censure. The main object of the book is, by examples taken chiefly from the works of contemporaries, to illustrate the truths, that art has fixed principles, of which any one may attain the knowledge who is not wanting in natural taste. Art, like poetry, is addressed to the world at large, not to a special jury of professional masters.* "*In many respects the truest critic we have.*"—LITERARY CHURCHMAN.

THE FIVE DAYS' ENTERTAINMENTS AT WENTWORTH GRANGE. A Book for Children. With Illustrations by ARTHUR HUGHES and Engraved Title-page by JEENS. Small 4to. cloth extra. 6s.

"*If you want a really good book for both sexes and all ages, buy this, as handsome a volume of tales as you'll find in all the market.*"—ATHENÆUM. "*Exquisite both in form and substance.*" —GUARDIAN.

LYRICAL POEMS. Extra fcap. 8vo. 6s.

"*A volume of pure quiet verse, sparkling with tender melodies, and alive with thoughts of genuine poetry. . . . Turn where we will throughout the volume, we find traces of beauty, tenderness, and truth; true poet's work, touched and refined by the master-hand of a real artist, who shows his genius even in trifles.*"—STANDARD.

ORIGINAL HYMNS. Third Edition, enlarged, 18mo. 1s. 6d.

"*So choice, so perfect, and so refined, so tender in feeling, and so scholarly in expression, that we look with special interest to everything that he gives us.*"—LITERARY CHURCHMAN.

GOLDEN TREASURY OF THE BEST SONGS AND LYRICS. Edited by F. T. PALGRAVE. See GOLDEN TREASURY SERIES.

Palgrave—*continued.*

SHAKESPEARE'S SONNETS AND SONGS. Edited by F. T. PALGRAVE. Gem Edition. With Vignette Title by JEENS. 3*s.* 6*d.*

"*For minute elegance no volume could possibly excel the 'Gem Edition.'*"—SCOTSMAN.

Parables.—TWELVE PARABLES OF OUR LORD. Illustrated in Colours from Sketches taken in the East by MCENIRY, with Frontispiece from a Picture by JOHN JELLICOE, and Illuminated Texts and Borders. Royal 4to. in Ornamental Binding. 16*s.*

The SCOTSMAN *calls this* "*one of the most superb books of the season.*" *The richly and tastefully illuminated borders are from the* Brevario Grimani, *in St. Mark's Library, Venice. The* TIMES *calls it* "*one of the most beautiful of modern pictorial works;*" *while the* GRAPHIC *says* "*nothing in this style, so good, has ever before been published.*"

Patmore.—THE ANGEL IN THE HOUSE. By COVENTRY PATMORE.

BOOK I. *The Betrothal;* BOOK II. *The Espousals;* BOOK III. *Faithful for Ever. The Victories of Love. Tamerton Church Tower.* Two Vols. Fcap. 8vo. 12*s.*

"*A style combining much of the homeliness of Crabbe, with sweeter music and a far higher range of thought.*"—TIMES. "*Its merit is more than sufficient to account for its success. . . . In its manly and healthy cheer, the 'Angel in the House' is an effectual protest against the morbid poetry of the age.*"—EDINBURGH REVIEW. "*We think his 'Angel in the House' would be a good wedding-gift to a bridegroom from his friends; though, whenever it is read with a right view of its aim, we believe it will be found itself, more or less, of an angel in the house.*"—FRASER'S MAGAZINE.

A New and Cheap Edition in One Vol. 18mo., *beautifully printed on toned paper, price* 2*s.* 6*d.*

Pember.—THE TRAGEDY OF LESBOS. A Dramatic Poem. By E. H PEMBER. Fcap. 8vo. 4*s.* 6*d.*

Founded upon the story of Sappho. "*He tells his story with dramatic force, and in language that often rises almost to grandeur.*"—ATHENÆUM.

Poole.—PICTURES OF COTTAGE LIFE IN THE WEST OF ENGLAND. By Margaret E. Poole. New and Cheaper Edition. With Frontispiece by R. Farren. Crown 8vo. 3s. 6d.

"*Charming stories of peasant life, written in something of George Eliot's style. . . . Her stories could not be other than they are, as literal as truth, as romantic as fiction, full of pathetic touches and strokes of genuine humour. . . . All the stories are studies of actual life, executed with no mean art.*"—Times.

Population of an Old Pear Tree. From the French of E. Van Bruyssel. Edited by the Author of "The Heir of Redclyffe." With Illustrations by Becker. Crown 8vo. gilt edges. 6s.

"*This is not a regular book of natural history, but a description of all the living creatures that came and went in a summer's day beneath an old pear tree, observed by eyes that had for the nonce become microscopic, recorded by a pen that finds dramas in everything, and illustrated by a dainty pencil. . . . We can hardly fancy anyone with a moderate turn for the curiosities of insect life, or for delicate French esprit, not being taken by these clever sketches.*"—Guardian. "*A whimsical and charming little book.*" —Athenæum.

Portfolio of Cabinet Pictures.—Oblong folio, price 42s.

This is a handsome portfolio containing faithfully executed and beautifully coloured reproductions of five well-known pictures:— "*Childe Harold's Pilgrimage*" *and* "*The Fighting Téméraire,*" *by J. M. W. Turner;* "*Crossing the Bridge,*" *by Sir W. A. Callcott;* "*The Cornfield,*" *by John Constable; and* "*A Landscape,*" *by Birket Foster. The* Daily News *says of them,* "*They are very beautifully executed, and might be framed and hung up on the wall, as creditable substitutes for the originals.*"

Raphael of Urbino and his Father Giovanni SANTI.—By J. D. Passavant, formerly Director of the Museum at Frankfort. Illustrated. Royal 8vo. cloth gilt, gilt edges. 31s. 6d.

> To the enlarged French edition of Herr Passavant's *Life of Raphael*, that painter's admirers have turned whenever they have sought for information; and it will doubtless remain for many years the best book of reference on all questions pertaining to the great painter. The present work consists of a translation of those parts of Passavant's volumes which are most likely to interest the general reader. Besides a complete life of Raphael it contains the valuable descriptions of all his known paintings, and the Chronological Index, which is of so much service to amateurs who wish to study the progressive character of his works. The illustrations, twenty in number, by Woodbury's new permanent process of photography, are from the finest engravings that could be procured, and have been chosen with the intention of giving examples of Raphael's various styles of painting. "There will be found in the volume almost all that the ordinary student or critic would require to learn."—ART JOURNAL. "It is most beautifully and profusely illustrated."—SATURDAY REVIEW.

Realmah.—By the Author of "Friends in Council." Crown 8vo. 6s.

Rhoades.—POEMS. By JAMES RHOADES. Fcap. 8vo. 4s. 6d.
> CONTENTS:—*Ode to Harmony; To the Spirit of Unrest; Ode to Winter; The Tunnel; To the Spirit of Beauty; Song of a Leaf; By the Rother; An Old Orchard; Love and Rest; The Flowers Surprised; On the Death of Artemus Ward; The Two Paths; The Ballad of Little Maisie; Sonnets.*

Richardson.—THE ILIAD OF THE EAST. A Selection of Legends drawn from Valmiki's Sanskrit Poem, "The Ramayana." By FREDERIKA RICHARDSON. Crown 8vo. 7s. 6d.

> "*It is impossible to read it without recognizing the value and interest of the Eastern epic. It is as fascinating as a fairy tale, this romantic poem of India.*"—GLOBE. "*A charming volume which at once enmeshes the reader in its snares.*"—ATHENÆUM.

Roby.—STORY OF A HOUSEHOLD, AND OTHER POEMS. By MARY K. ROBY. Fcap. 8vo. 5s.

Rogers.—Works by J. E. Rogers :—

RIDICULA REDIVIVA. Old Nursery Rhymes. Illustrated in Colours, with Ornamental Cover. Crown 4to. 6s.

"*The most splendid, and at the same time the most really meritorious of the books specially intended for children, that we have seen.*"— SPECTATOR. "*These large bright pictures will attract children to really good and honest artistic work, and that ought not to be an indifferent consideration with parents who propose to educate their children.*"—PALL MALL GAZETTE.

MORES RIDICULI. Old Nursery Rhymes. Illustrated in Colours, with Ornamental Cover. Crown 4to. 6s.

"*These world-old rhymes have never had and need never wish for a better pictorial setting than Mr. Rogers has given them.*"— TIMES. "*Nothing could be quainter or more absurdly comical than most of the pictures, which are all carefully executed and beautifully coloured.*"—GLOBE.

Rossetti.—Works by CHRISTINA ROSSETTI :—

GOBLIN MARKET, AND OTHER POEMS. With two Designs by D. G. ROSSETTI. Second Edition. Fcap. 8vo. 5s.

"*She handles her little marvel with that rare poetic discrimination which neither exhausts it of its simple wonders by pushing symbolism too far, nor keeps those wonders in the merely fabulous and capricious stage. In fact, she has produced a true children's poem, which is far more delightful to the mature than to children, though it would be delightful to all.*"—SPECTATOR.

THE PRINCE'S PROGRESS, AND OTHER POEMS. With two Designs by D. G. ROSSETTI. Fcap. 8vo. 6s.

"*Miss Rossetti's poems are of the kind which recalls Shelley's definition of Poetry as the record of the best and happiest moments of the best and happiest minds. . . . They are like the piping of a bird on the spray in the sunshine, or the quaint singing with which a child amuses itself when it forgets that anybody is listening.*"— SATURDAY REVIEW.

Runaway (The). A Story for the Young. By the Author of "Mrs. Jerningham's Journal." With Illustrations by J. LAWSON. Globe 8vo. gilt. 4s. 6d.

C

Ruth and her Friends. A Story for Girls. With a Frontispiece. Fourth Edition. Royal 16mo. 3s. 6d.

"*We wish all the school girls and home-taught girls in the land had the opportunity of reading it.*"—NONCONFORMIST.

Scouring of the White Horse; or, the Long VACATION RAMBLE OF A LONDON CLERK. Illustrated by DOYLE. Imp. 16mo. Cheaper Issue. 3s. 6d.

"*A glorious tale of summer joy.*"—FREEMAN. "*There is a genial hearty life about the book.*"—JOHN BULL. "*The execution is excellent. . . . Like 'Tom Brown's School Days,' the 'White Horse' gives the reader a feeling of gratitude and personal esteem towards the author.*"—SATURDAY REVIEW.

Seeley (Professor).—LECTURES AND ESSAYS. By J. R. SEELEY, M.A. Professor of Modern History in the University of Cambridge. 8vo. 10s. 6d.

CONTENTS:—*Roman Imperialism:* 1. *The Great Roman Revolution;* 2. *The Proximate Cause of the Fall of the Roman Empire;* 3. *The Later Empire.—Milton's Political Opinions — Milton's Poetry—Elementary Principles in Art—Liberal Education in Universities— English in Schools—The Church as a Teacher of Morality—The Teaching of Politics: an Inaugural Lecture delivered at Cambridge.* "*He is the master of a clear and pleasant style, great facility of expression, and a considerable range of illustration. . . . The criticism is always acute, the description always graphic and continuous, and the matter of each essay is carefully arranged with a view to unity of effect.*"—SPECTATOR. "*His book will be full of interest to all thoughtful readers.*"—PALL MALL GAZETTE.

Shairp (Principal).—KILMAHOE, a Highland Pastoral, with other Poems. By JOHN CAMPBELL SHAIRP, Principal of the United College, St. Andrews. Fcap. 8vo. 5s.

"*Kilmahoe is a Highland Pastoral, redolent of the warm soft air of the western lochs and moors, sketched out with remarkable grace and picturesqueness.*"—SATURDAY REVIEW.

Shakespeare.—The Works of WILLIAM SHAKESPEARE. Cambridge Edition. Edited by W. GEORGE CLARK, M.A. and W. ALDIS WRIGHT, M.A. Nine vols. 8vo. Cloth. 4*l*. 14*s*. 6*d*.

This, now acknowledged to be the standard edition of Shakespeare, is the result of many years' study and research on the part of the accomplished Editors, assisted by the suggestions and contributions of Shakespearian students in all parts of the country. The following are the distinctive characteristics of this edition:—1. *The text is based on a thorough collation of the four Folios, and of all the Quarto editions of the separate plays, and of subsequent editions and commentaries.* 2. *All the results of this collation are given in notes at the foot of the page, together with the conjectural emendations collected and suggested by the Editors, or furnished by their correspondents, so as to give the reader a complete view of the existing materials out of which the text has been constructed, or may be amended.* 3. *Where a quarto edition differs materially from the received text, the text of the quarto is printed* literatim *in a smaller type after the received text.* 4. *The lines in each scene are numbered separately, so as to facilitate reference.* 5. *At the end of each play a few notes, critical, explanatory, and illustrative, are added.* 6. *The Poems, edited on a similar plan, are printed at the end of the Dramatic Works. The Preface contains some notes on Shakespearian Grammar, Spelling, Metre, and Punctuation, and a history of all the chief editions from the Poet's time to the present. The* GUARDIAN *calls it an "excellent, and, to the student, almost indispensable edition;" and the* EXAMINER *calls it "an unrivalled edition."*

Shakespeare's Tempest. Edited with Glossarial and Explanatory Notes, by the Rev. J. M. JEPHSON. Second Edition. 18mo. 1*s*.

This is an edition for use in schools. The introduction treats briefly of the value of language, the fable of the play and other points. The notes are intended to teach the student to analyse every obscure sentence and trace out the logical sequence of the poet's thoughts; to point out the rules of Shakespeare's versification; to explain obsolete words and meanings; and to guide the student's taste by directing his attention to such passages as seem especially worthy of note for their poetical beauty or truth to nature. The text is in the main founded upon that of the first collected edition of Shakespeare's plays.

Smith.—POEMS. By CATHERINE BARNARD SMITH. Fcap. 8vo. 5s.

"*Wealthy in feeling, meaning, finish, and grace; not without passion, which is suppressed, but the keener for that.*"—ATHENÆUM.

Smith (Rev. Walter).—HYMNS OF CHRIST AND THE CHRISTIAN LIFE. By the Rev. WALTER C. SMITH, M.A. Fcap. 8vo. 6s.

"*These are among the sweetest sacred poems we have read for a long time. With no profuse imagery, expressing a range of feeling and expression by no means uncommon, they are true and elevated, and their pathos is profound and simple.*"—NONCONFORMIST.

Spring Songs. By a WEST HIGHLANDER. With a Vignette Illustration by GOURLAY STEELE. Fcap. 8vo. 1s. 6d.

"*Without a trace of affectation or sentimentalism, these utterances are perfectly simple and natural, profoundly human and profoundly true.*"—DAILY NEWS.

Stephen (C. E.)—THE SERVICE OF THE POOR; being an Inquiry into the Reasons for and against the Establishment of Religious Sisterhoods for Charitable Purposes. By CAROLINE EMILIA STEPHEN. Crown 8vo. 6s. 6d.

Miss Stephen defines religious Sisterhoods as "associations, the organization of which is based upon the assumption that works of charity are either acts of worship in themselves, or means to an end, that end being the spiritual welfare of the objects or the performers of those works." Arguing from that point of view, she devotes the first part of her volume to a brief history of religious associations, taking as specimens—I. The Deaconesses of the Primitive Church; II. the Béguines; III. the Third Order of S. Francis; IV. the Sisters of Charity of S. Vincent de Paul; V. the Deaconesses of Modern Germany. In the second part, Miss Stephen attempts to show what are the real wants met by Sisterhoods, to what extent the same wants may be effectually met by the organization of corresponding institutions on a secular basis, and what are the reasons for endeavouring to do so. "It touches incidentally and with much wisdom and tenderness on so many of the relations of women, par-

ticularly *of single women, with society, that it may be read with advantage by many who have never thought of entering a Sisterhood."*—SPECTATOR.

Stephens (J. B.)—CONVICT ONCE. A Poem. By J. BRUNTON STEPHENS. Extra fcap. 8vo. 3s. 6d.

A tale of sin and sorrow, purporting to be the confession of Magdalen Power, a convict first, and then a teacher in one of the Australian Settlements; the narrative is supposed to be written by Hyacinth, a pupil of Magdalen Power, and the victim of her jealousy. The metre of the poem is the same as that of Longfellow's "Evangeline." "It is as far more interesting than ninety-nine novels out of a hundred, as it is superior to them in power, worth, and beauty. We should most strongly advise everybody to read 'Convict Once.'"—WESTMINSTER REVIEW.

Stray Leaves. By C. E. M. Extra fcap. 8vo. 3s. 6d. Contents:—"His and Mine"—"Night and Day"—"One of Many," &c.

This little volume consists of a number of poems, mostly of a genuinely devotional character. "They are for the most part so exquisitely sweet and delicate as to be quite a marvel of composition. They are worthy of being laid up in the recesses of the heart, and recalled to memory from time to time."—ILLUSTRATED LONDON NEWS.

Streets and Lanes of a City: Being the Reminiscences of AMY DUTTON. With a Preface by the BISHOP OF SALISBURY. Second and Cheaper Edition. Globe 8vo. 2s. 6d.

This little volume records, to use the words of the Bishop of Salisbury, "a portion of the experience, selected out of overflowing materials, of two ladies, during several years of devoted work as district parochial visitors in a large population in the north of England." Every incident narrated is absolutely true, and only the names of the persons introduced have been (necessarily) changed. The "Reminiscences of Amy Dutton" serve to illustrate the line of argument adopted by Miss Stephen in her work on "the Service of the Poor," because they show that as in one aspect the lady visitor may be said to be a link between rich and poor, in another she helps to blend the "religious" life with the "secular," and in both does service of extreme value to the Church and Nation. "One of the most really striking books that has ever come before us."—LITERARY CHURCHMAN.

Symonds (J. A., M.D.)—MISCELLANIES. By JOHN ADDINGTON SYMONDS, M.D. Selected and Edited, with an Introductory Memoir, by his Son. 8vo. 7s. 6d.

> *The late Dr. Symonds, of Bristol, was a man of singularly versatile and elegant as well as powerful and scientific intellect. In order to make this selection from his many works generally interesting, the editor has confined himself to works of pure literature, and to such scientific studies as had a general philosophical or social interest. Among the general subjects are articles on the Principles of Beauty, on Knowledge, and a Life of Dr. Pritchard; among the Scientific Studies are papers on Sleep and Dreams, Apparitions, the Relations between Mind and Muscle, Habit, etc.; there are several papers on the Social and Political Aspects of Medicine; and a few Poems and Translations, selected from a great number of equal merit, have been inserted at the end, as specimens of the lighter literary recreations which occupied the intervals of leisure in a long and laborious life. "Mr. Symonds has certainly done right in gathering together what his father left behind him."*—SATURDAY REVIEW.

Thring.—SCHOOL SONGS. A Collection of Songs for Schools. With the Music arranged for four Voices. Edited by the Rev. E. THRING and H. RICCIUS. Folio. 7s. 6d.

> *There is a tendency in schools to stereotype the forms of life. Any genial solvent is valuable. Games do much; but games do not penetrate to domestic life, and are much limited by age. Music supplies the want. The collection includes the "Agnus Dei," Tennyson's "Light Brigade," Macaulay's "Ivry," etc. among other pieces.*

Tom Brown's School Days.—By AN OLD BOY.
Golden Treasury Edition, 4s. 6d. People's Edition, 2s.
With Sixty Illustrations, by A. HUGHES and SYDNEY HALL, Square, cloth extra, gilt edges. 10s. 6d.
With Seven Illustrations by the same Artists, Crown 8vo. 6s.

> *"We have read and re-read this book with unmingled pleasure.... We have carefully guarded ourselves against any tampering with our critical sagacity, and yet have been compelled again and again to exclaim, Bene! Optime!"*—LONDON QUARTERLY REVIEW.
> *"An exact picture of the bright side of a Rugby boy's experience,*

told with a life, a spirit, and a fond minuteness of detail and recollection which is infinitely honourable to the author."—EDINBURGH REVIEW. "The most famous boy's book in the language."—DAILY NEWS.

Tom Brown at Oxford.—New Edition. With Illustrations Crown 8vo. 6s.

"*In no other work that we can call to mind are the finer qualities of the English gentleman more happily portrayed.*"—DAILY NEWS. "*A book of great power and truth.*"—NATIONAL REVIEW.

Trench.—Works by R. CHENEVIX TRENCH, D.D., Archbishop of Dublin. (For other Works by this Author, see THEOLOGICAL, HISTORICAL, and PHILOSOPHICAL CATALOGUES.)

POEMS. Collected and arranged anew. Fcap. 8vo. 7s. 6d.

ELEGIAC POEMS. Third Edition. Fcap. 8vo. 2s. 6d.

CALDERON'S LIFE'S A DREAM: The Great Theatre of the World. With an Essay on his Life and Genius. Fcap. 8vo. 4s. 6d.

HOUSEHOLD BOOK OF ENGLISH POETRY. Selected and arranged, with Notes, by Archbishop TRENCH. Second Edition. Extra fcap. 8vo. 5s. 6d.

This volume is called a "Household Book," by this name implying that it is a book for all—that there is nothing in it to prevent it from being confidently placed in the hands of every member of the household. Specimens of all classes of poetry are given, including selections from living authors. The editor has aimed to produce a book "which the emigrant, finding room for little not absolutely necessary, might yet find room for in his trunk, and the traveller in his knapsack, and that on some narrow shelves where there are few books this might be one." " The Archbishop has conferred in this delightful volume an important gift on the whole English-speaking population of the world."—PALL MALL GAZETTE.

SACRED LATIN POETRY, Chiefly Lyrical. Selected and arranged for Use. By Archbishop TRENCH. Second Edition, Corrected and Improved. Fcap. 8vo. 7s.

> "*The aim of the present volume is to offer to members of our English Church a collection of the best sacred Latin poetry, such as they shall be able entirely and heartily to accept and approve—a collection, that is, in which they shall not be evermore liable to be offended, and to have the current of their sympathies checked, by coming upon that which, however beautiful as poetry, out of higher respects they must reject and condemn—in which, too, they shall not fear that snares are being laid for them, to entangle them unawares in admiration for aught which is inconsistent with their faith and fealty to their own spiritual mother.*"—PREFACE.

JUSTIN MARTYR, AND OTHER POEMS. Fifth Edition. Fcap. 8vo. 6s.

Trollope (Anthony). — SIR HARRY HOTSPUR OF HUMBLETHWAITE. By ANTHONY TROLLOPE, Author of "Framley Parsonage," etc. Cheap Edition. Globe 8vo. 2s. 6d.

> The TIMES says: "*In this novel we are glad to recognize a return to what we must call Mr. Trollope's old form. The characters are drawn with vigour and boldness, and the book may do good to many readers of both sexes.*" The ATHENÆUM remarks: "*No reader who begins to read this book is likely to lay it down until the last page is turned. This brilliant novel appears to us decidedly more successful than any other of Mr. Trollope's shorter stories.*"

Turner.—Works by the Rev. CHARLES TENNYSON TURNER :—

SONNETS. Dedicated to his Brother, the Poet Laureate. Fcap. 8vo. 4s. 6d.

> "*The Sonnets are dedicated to Mr. Tennyson by his brother, and have, independently of their merits, an interest of association. They both love to write in simple expressive Saxon; both love to touch their imagery in epithets rather than in formal similes; both have a delicate perception of rhythmical movement, and thus Mr. Turner has occasional lines which, for phrase and music, might be ascribed to his brother. . . He knows the haunts of the wild rose, the shady nooks where light quivers through the leaves, the ruralities, in short, of the land of imagination.*"—ATHENÆUM.

SMALL TABLEAUX. Fcap. 8vo. 4s. 6d.

> "*These brief poems have not only a peculiar kind of interest for the student of English poetry, but are intrinsically delightful, and*

will reward a careful and frequent perusal. Full of naïveté, piety, love, and knowledge of natural objects, and each expressing a single and generally a simple subject by means of minute and original pictorial touches, these Sonnets have a place of their own."—PALL MALL GAZETTE.

Vittoria Colonna.—LIFE AND POEMS. By MRS. HENRY ROSCOE. Crown 8vo. 9s.

The life of Vittoria Colonna, the celebrated Marchesa di Pescara, has received but cursory notice from any English writer, though in every history of Italy her name is mentioned with great honour among the poets of the sixteenth century. "In three hundred and fifty years," says her biographer, Visconti, "there has been no other Italian lady who can be compared to her." "It is written with good taste, with quick and intelligent sympathy, occasionally with a real freshness and charm of style."—PALL MALL GAZETTE.

Volunteer's Scrap Book. By the Author of "The Cambridge Scrap Book." Crown 4to. 7s. 6d.

"A genial and clever caricaturist in whom we may often perceive through small details that he has as proper a sense of the graceful as of the ludicrous. The author might be and probably is a Volunteer himself, so kindly is the mirth he makes of all the incidents and phrases of the drill-ground."—EXAMINER.

Wandering Willie. By the Author of "Effie's Friends," and "John Hatherton." Third Edition. Crown 8vo. 6s.

"This is an idyll of rare truth and beauty.... The story is simple and touching, the style of extraordinary delicacy, precision, and picturesqueness.... A charming gift-book for young ladies not yet promoted to novels, and will amply repay those of their elders who may give an hour to its perusal."—DAILY NEWS.

Webster.—Works by AUGUSTA WEBSTER :—

"If Mrs. Webster only remains true to herself, she will assuredly take a higher rank as a poet than any woman has yet done."—WESTMINSTER REVIEW.

Webster.—*continued.*

DRAMATIC STUDIES. Extra fcap. 8vo. 5s.

"*A volume as strongly marked by perfect taste as by poetic power.*"—NONCONFORMIST.

A WOMAN SOLD, AND OTHER POEMS. Crown 8vo. 7s. 6d.

"*Mrs. Webster has shown us that she is able to draw admirably from the life; that she can observe with subtlety, and render her observations with delicacy; that she can impersonate complex conceptions and venture into which few living writers can follow her.*"—GUARDIAN.

PORTRAITS. Second Edition. Extra fcap. 8vo. 3s. 6d.

"*Mrs. Webster's poems exhibit simplicity and tenderness . . . her taste is perfect . . . This simplicity is combined with a subtlety of thought, feeling, and observation which demand that attention which only real lovers of poetry are apt to bestow.*"—WESTMINSTER REVIEW.

PROMETHEUS BOUND OF ÆSCHYLUS. Literally translated into English Verse. Extra fcap. 8vo. 3s. 6d.

"*Closeness and simplicity combined with literary skill.*"— ATHENÆUM. "*Mrs. Webster's 'Dramatic Studies' and 'Translation of Prometheus' have won for her an honourable place among our female poets. She writes with remarkable vigour and dramatic realization, and bids fair to be the most successful claimant of Mrs. Browning's mantle.*"—BRITISH QUARTERLY REVIEW.

MEDEA OF EURIPIDES. Literally translated into English Verse. Extra fcap. 8vo. 3s. 6d.

"*Mrs. Webster's translation surpasses our utmost expectations. It is a photograph of the original without any of that harshness which so often accompanies a photograph.*"—WESTMINSTER REVIEW.

THE AUSPICIOUS DAY. A Dramatic Poem. Extra fcap. 8vo. 5s.

Westminster Plays. Lusus Alteri Westmonasterienses, Sive Prologi et Epilogi ad Fabulas in S^{ti} Petri Collegio : actas qui Exstabant collecti et justa quoad licuit annorum serie ordinati, quibus accedit Declamationum quæ vocantur et Epigrammatum Delectus. Curantibus J. MURE, A.M., H. BULL, A.M., C. B. SCOTT, B.D. 8vo. 12s. 6d.

IDEM.—Pars Secunda, 1820—1864. Quibus accedit Epigrammatum Delectus. 8vo. 15s.

When I was a Little Girl. STORIES FOR CHILDREN.
By the Author of "St. Olave's." Fourth Edition. Extra fcap. 8vo. 4s. 6d. With Eight Illustrations by L. FRÖLICH.

"*At the head, and a long way ahead, of all books for girls, we place 'When I was a Little Girl.'*"—TIMES. "*It is one of the choicest morsels of child-biography which we have met with.*"—NONCONFORMIST.

Wollaston.—LYRA DEVONIENSIS. By T. V. WOLLASTON, M.A. Fcap. 8vo. 3s. 6d.

"*It is the work of a man of refined taste, of deep religious sentiment, a true artist, and a good Christian.*"—CHURCH TIMES.

Woolner.—MY BEAUTIFUL LADY. By THOMAS WOOLNER.
With a Vignette by ARTHUR HUGHES. Third Edition. Fcap. 8vo. 5s.

"*It is clearly the product of no idle hour, but a highly-conceived and faithfully-executed task, self-imposed, and prompted by that inward yearning to utter great thoughts, and a wealth of passionate feeling, which is poetic genius. No man can read this poem without being struck by the fitness and finish of the workmanship, so to speak, as well as by the chastened and unpretending loftiness of thought which pervades the whole.*"—GLOBE.

Words from the Poets. Selected by the Editor of "Rays of Sunlight." With a Vignette and Frontispiece. 18mo. limp., 1s.

"*The selection aims at popularity, and deserves it.*"—GUARDIAN.

Wyatt (Sir M. Digby).—FINE ART: a Sketch of its History, Theory, Practice, and application to Industry. A Course of Lectures delivered before the University of Cambridge. By Sir M. DIGBY WYATT, M.A. Slade Professor of Fine Art. 8vo. 10s. 6d.

"*An excellent handbook for the student of art.*"—GRAPHIC. "*The book abounds in valuable matter, and will therefore be read with pleasure and profit by lovers of art.*"—DAILY NEWS.

Yonge (C. M.)—Works by CHARLOTTE M. YONGE. (See also CATALOGUE OF WORKS IN HISTORY, and EDUCATIONAL CATALOGUE.)

THE HEIR OF REDCLYFFE. Nineteenth Edition. With Illustrations. Crown 8vo. 6s.

HEARTSEASE. Twelfth Edition. With Illustrations. Crown 8vo. 6s.

THE DAISY CHAIN. Eleventh Edition. With Illustrations. Crown 8vo. 6s.

THE TRIAL: MORE LINKS OF THE DAISY CHAIN. Sixth Edition. With Illustrations. Crown 8vo. 6s.

DYNEVOR TERRACE. Fifth Edition. Crown 8vo. 6s.

HOPES AND FEARS. Fourth Edition. Crown 8vo. 6s.

THE YOUNG STEPMOTHER. Third Edition. Crown 8vo. 6s.

CLEVER WOMAN OF THE FAMILY. Third Edition. Crown 8vo. 6s.

THE DOVE IN THE EAGLE'S NEST. Second Edition. Crown 8vo. 6s.

"*We think the authoress of 'The Heir of Redclyffe' has surpassed her previous efforts in this illuminated chronicle of the olden time.*"—BRITISH QUARTERLY.

THE CAGED LION. Illustrated. Second Edition. Crown 8vo. 6s.

"*Prettily and tenderly written, and will with young people especially be a great favourite.*"—DAILY NEWS. "*Everybody should read this.*"—LITERARY CHURCHMAN.

THE CHAPLET OF PEARLS; OR, THE WHITE AND BLACK RIBAUMONT. Crown 8vo. 6s. New Edition.

Yonge (C. M.)—*continued.*

"*Miss Yonge has brought a lofty aim as well as high art to the construction of a story which may claim a place among the best efforts in historical romance.*"—MORNING POST. "*The plot, in truth, is of the very first order of merit.*"—SPECTATOR. "*We have seldom read a more charming story.*"—GUARDIAN.

THE PRINCE AND THE PAGE. A Tale of the Last Crusade. Illustrated. 18mo. 3s. 6d.

"*A tale which, we are sure, will give pleasure to many others besides the young people for whom it is specially intended. . . . This extremely prettily-told story does not require the guarantee afforded by the name of the author of 'The Heir of Redclyffe' on the title-page to ensure its becoming a universal favourite.*"—DUBLIN EVENING MAIL.

THE LANCES OF LYNWOOD. New Edition, with Coloured Illustrations. 18mo. 4s. 6d.

"*The illustrations are very spirited and rich in colour, and the story can hardly fail to charm the youthful reader*"—MANCHESTER EXAMINER.

THE LITTLE DUKE: RICHARD THE FEARLESS. New Edition. Illustrated. 18mo. 3s. 6d.

A STOREHOUSE OF STORIES. First and Second Series. Globe 8vo. 3s. 6d. each.

CONTENTS OF FIRST SERIES:—History of Philip Quarll—Goody Twoshoes—The Governess—Jemima Placid—The Perambulations of a Mouse—The Village School—The Little Queen—History of Little Jack.

"*Miss Yonge has done great service to the infantry of this generation by putting these eleven stories of sage simplicity within their reach.*" —BRITISH QUARTERLY REVIEW.

CONTENTS OF SECOND SERIES:—Family Stories—Elements of Morality—A Puzzle for a Curious Girl—Blossoms of Morality.

A BOOK OF GOLDEN DEEDS OF ALL TIMES AND ALL COUNTRIES. Gathered and Narrated Anew. New Edition, with Twenty Illustrations by FRÖLICH. Crown 8vo. cloth gilt. 6s. (See also GOLDEN TREASURY SERIES). Cheap Edition. 1s.

Yonge (C. M.)—*continued.*

"*We have seen no prettier gift-book for a long time, and none which, both for its cheapness and the spirit in which it has been compiled, is more deserving of praise.*"—ATHENÆUM.

LITTLE LUCY'S WONDERFUL GLOBE Pictured by FRÖLICH, and narrated by CHARLOTTE M. YONGE. Second Edition. Crown 4to. cloth gilt. 6s.

Miss Yonge's wonderful "knack" of instructive story-telling to children is well known. In this volume, in a manner which cannot but prove interesting to all boys and girls, she manages to convey a wonderful amount of information concerning most of the countries of the world; in this she is considerably aided by the twenty-four telling pictures of Mr. Frölich. "'Lucy's Wonderful Globe' is capital, and will give its youthful readers more idea of foreign countries and customs than any number of books of geography or travel."—GRAPHIC.

CAMEOS FROM ENGLISH HISTORY. From ROLLO to EDWARD II. Extra fcap. 8vo. 5s. Second Edition, enlarged. 5s.

A SECOND SERIES. THE WARS IN FRANCE. Extra fcap. 8vo. 5s.

The endeavour has not been to chronicle facts, but to put together a series of pictures of persons and events, so as to arrest the attention, and give some individuality and distinctness to the recollection, by gathering together details at the most memorable moments. The "Cameos" are intended as a book for young people just beyond the elementary histories of England, and able to enter in some degree into the real spirit of events, and to be struck with characters and scenes presented in some relief. "Instead of dry details," says the NONCONFORMIST, "*we have living pictures, faithful, vivid, and striking.*"

P's AND Q's: Or, THE QUESTION OF PUTTING UPON. With Illustrations by C. O. MURRAY. Globe 8vo. cloth gilt. 4s. 6d.

Young.—MEMOIR OF CHARLES MAYNE YOUNG,

Tragedian. With Extracts from his Son's Journal. By JULIAN CHARLES YOUNG, M.A., Rector of Ilmington. New and Cheaper Edition. Crown 8vo. 7s. 6d. With Portraits and Sketches.

"*There is hardly a page of it which was not worth printing. There is hardly a line which has not some kind of interest attaching to it.*"—GUARDIAN. "*In this budget of anecdotes, fables, ana gossip, old and new, relative to Scott, Moore, Chalmers, Coleridge, Wordsworth, Croker, Mathews, the Third and Fourth Georges, Bowles, Beckford, Lockhart, Wellington, Peel, Louis Napoleon, D'Orsay, Dickens, Thackeray, Louis Blanc, Gibson, Constable, and Stanfield (the list might be much extended), the reader must be hard indeed to please who cannot find entertainment.*"—PALL MALL GAZETTE.

MACMILLAN'S
GOLDEN TREASURY SERIES.

UNIFORMLY printed in 18mo., with Vignette Titles by Sir NOEL PATON, T. WOOLNER, W. HOLMAN HUNT, J. E. MILLAIS, ARTHUR HUGHES, &c. Engraved on Steel by JEENS. Bound in extra cloth, 4s. 6d. each volume. Also kept in morocco and calf bindings.

> *"Messrs. Macmillan have, in their Golden Treasury Series, especially provided editions of standard works, volumes of selected poetry, and original compositions, which entitle this series to be called classical. Nothing can be better than the literary execution, nothing more elegant than the material workmanship."* — BRITISH QUARTERLY REVIEW.

The Golden Treasury of the Best Songs and LYRICAL POEMS IN THE ENGLISH LANGUAGE. Selected and arranged, with Notes, by FRANCIS TURNER PALGRAVE.

> *"This delightful little volume, the Golden Treasury, which contains many of the best original lyrical pieces and songs in our language, grouped with care and skill, so as to illustrate each other like the pictures in a well-arranged gallery."* — QUARTERLY REVIEW.

The Children's Garland from the best Poets. Selected and arranged by COVENTRY PATMORE.

> *"It includes specimens of all the great masters in the art of poetry, selected with the matured judgment of a man concentrated on obtaining insight into the feelings and tastes of childhood, and*

desirous to awaken its finest impulses, to cultivate its keenest sensibilities."—MORNING POST.

The Book of Praise. From the Best English Hymn Writers. Selected and arranged by Sir ROUNDELL PALMER. *A New and Enlarged Edition.*

"*All previous compilations of this kind must undeniably for the present give place to the Book of Praise. . . . The selection has been made throughout with sound judgment and critical taste. The pains involved in this compilation must have been immense, embracing, as it does, every writer of note in this special province of English literature, and ranging over the most widely divergent tracks of religious thought.*"—SATURDAY REVIEW.

The Fairy Book; the Best Popular Fairy Stories. Selected and rendered anew by the Author of "JOHN HALIFAX, GENTLEMAN."

"*A delightful selection, in a delightful external form; full of the physical splendour and vast opulence of proper fairy tales.*"—SPECTATOR.

The Ballad Book. A Selection of the Choicest British Ballads. Edited by WILLIAM ALLINGHAM.

"*His taste as a judge of old poetry will be found, by all acquainted with the various readings of old English ballads, true enough to justify his undertaking so critical a task.*"—SATURDAY REVIEW.

The Jest Book. The Choicest Anecdotes and Sayings. Selected and arranged by MARK LEMON.

"*The fullest and best jest book that has yet appeared.*"—SATURDAY REVIEW.

Bacon's Essays and Colours of Good and Evil. With Notes and Glossarial Index. By W. ALDIS WRIGHT, M.A.

"*The beautiful little edition of Bacon's Essays, now before us, does credit to the taste and scholarship of Mr. Aldis Wright. . . . It puts the reader in possession of all the essential literary facts and chronology necessary for reading the Essays in connection with Bacon's life and times.*"—SPECTATOR. "*By far the most complete as well as the most elegant edition we possess.*"—WESTMINSTER REVIEW.

D

The Pilgrim's Progress from this World to that which is to come. By JOHN BUNYAN.

"*A beautiful and scholarly reprint.*"—SPECTATOR.

The Sunday Book of Poetry for the Young. Selected and arranged by C. F. ALEXANDER.

"*A well-selected volume of Sacred Poetry.*"—SPECTATOR.

A Book of Golden Deeds of All Times and All Countries. Gathered and narrated anew. By the Author of "THE HEIR OF REDCLYFFE."

"*. . . To the young, for whom it is especially intended, as a most interesting collection of thrilling tales well told; and to their elders, as a useful handbook of reference, and a pleasant one to take up when their wish is to while away a weary half-hour. We have seen no prettier gift-book for a long time.*"—ATHENÆUM.

The Poetical Works of Robert Burns. Edited, with Biographical Memoir, Notes, and Glossary, by ALEXANDER SMITH. Two Vols.

"*Beyond all question this is the most beautiful edition of Burns yet out.*"—EDINBURGH DAILY REVIEW.

The Adventures of Robinson Crusoe. Edited from the Original Edition by J. W. CLARK, M.A., Fellow of Trinity College, Cambridge.

"*Mutilated and modified editions of this English classic are so much the rule, that a cheap and pretty copy of it, rigidly exact to the original, will be a prize to many book-buyers.*"—EXAMINER.

The Republic of Plato. TRANSLATED into ENGLISH, with Notes by J. Ll. DAVIES, M.A. and D. J. VAUGHAN, M.A.

"*A dainty and cheap little edition.*"—EXAMINER.

The Song Book. Words and Tunes from the best Poets and Musicians. Selected and arranged by JOHN HULLAH, Professor of Vocal Music in King's College, London.

"*A choice collection of the sterling songs of England, Scotland, and Ireland, with the music of each prefixed to the words. How much true wholesome pleasure such a book can diffuse, and will diffuse, we trust, through many thousand families.*"—EXAMINER.

La Lyre Française. Selected and arranged, with Notes, by GUSTAVE MASSON, French Master in Harrow School.

A selection of the best French songs and lyrical pieces.

Tom Brown's School Days. By AN OLD BOY.

"*A perfect gem of a book. The best and most healthy book about boys for boys that ever was written.*"—ILLUSTRATED TIMES.

A Book of Worthies. Gathered from the Old Histories and written anew by the Author of "THE HEIR OF REDCLYFFE." With Vignette.

"*An admirable addition to an admirable series.*"—WESTMINSTER REVIEW.

A Book of Golden Thoughts. By HENRY ATTWELL, Knight of the Order of the Oak Crown.

"*Mr. Attwell has produced a book of rare value .... Happily it is small enough to be carried about in the pocket, and of such a companion it would be difficult to weary.*"—PALL MALL GAZETTE.

Guesses at Truth. By TWO BROTHERS. New Edition.

The Cavalier and his Lady. Selections from the Works of the First Duke and Duchess of Newcastle. With an Introductory Essay by EDWARD JENKINS, Author of "Ginx's Baby," &c. 18mo. 4s. 6d.

MACMILLAN'S

GLOBE LIBRARY.

Beautifully printed on toned paper and bound in cloth extra, gilt edges, price 4s. 6d. each; in cloth plain, 3s. 6d. Also kept in a variety of calf and morocco bindings at moderate prices.

BOOKS, Wordsworth says, are

"the spirit breathed
By dead men to their kind;"

and the aim of the publishers of the Globe Library has been to make it possible for the universal kin of English-speaking men to hold communion with the loftiest "spirits of the mighty dead;" to put within the reach of all classes *complete* and *accurate* editions, carefully and clearly printed upon the best paper, in a convenient form, at a moderate price, of the works of the MASTER-MINDS OF ENGLISH LITERATURE, and occasionally of foreign literature in an attractive English dress.

The Editors, by their scholarship and special study of their authors, are competent to afford every assistance to readers of all kinds: this assistance is rendered by original biographies, glossaries of unusual or obsolete words, and critical and explanatory notes.

The publishers hope, therefore, that these Globe Editions may prove worthy of acceptance by all classes wherever the English Language is spoken, and by their universal circulation justify their distinctive epithet; while at the same time they spread and nourish a common sympathy with nature's most "finely touched" spirits, and thus help a little to "make the whole world kin."

> *The* SATURDAY REVIEW *says:* "*The Globe Editions are admirable for their scholarly editing, their typographical excellence, their compendious form, and their cheapness.*" *The* BRITISH QUARTERLY REVIEW *says:* "*In compendiousness, elegance, and scholarliness, the Globe Editions of Messrs. Macmillan surpass any popular series of our classics hitherto given to the public. As near an approach to miniature perfection as has ever been made.*"

Shakespeare's Complete Works. Edited by W. G. CLARK, M.A., and W. ALDIS WRIGHT, M.A., of Trinity College, Cambridge, Editors of the "Cambridge Shakespeare." With Glossary. pp. 1,075. Price 3s. 6d.

> *This edition aims at presenting a perfectly reliable text of the complete works of "the foremost man in all literature." The text is essentially the same as that of the "Cambridge Shakespeare." Appended is a Glossary containing the meaning of every word in the text which is either obsolete or is used in an antiquated or unusual sense. This, combined with the method used to indicate corrupted readings, serves to a great extent the purpose of notes. The* ATHENÆUM *says this edition is "a marvel of beauty, cheapness, and compactness. . . . For the busy man, above all for the working student, this is the best of all existing Shakespeares." And the* PALL MALL GAZETTE *observes:* "*To have produced th. complete works of the world's greatest poet in such a form, and at a price within the reach of every one, is of itself almost sufficient to give the publishers a claim to be considered public benefactors.*"

Spenser's Complete Works. Edited from the Original Editions and Manuscripts, by R. MORRIS, with a Memoir by J. W. HALES, M.A. With Glossary. pp. lv., 736. Price 3s. 6d.

The text of the poems has been reprinted from the earliest known editions, carefully collated with subsequent ones, most of which were published in the poet's lifetime. Spenser's only prose work, his sagacious and interesting " View of the State of Ireland," has been re-edited from three manuscripts belonging to the British Museum. A complete Glossary and a list of all the most important various readings serve to a large extent the purpose of notes explanatory and critical. An exhaustive general Index and a useful " Index of first lines" precede the poems; and in an Appendix are given Spenser's Letters to Gabriel Harvey. " Worthy—and higher praise it needs not—of the beautiful ' Globe Series.' The work is edited with all the care so noble a poet deserves."—DAILY NEWS.

Sir Walter Scott's Poetical Works. Edited with a Biographical and Critical Memoir by FRANCIS TURNER PALGRAVE, and copious Notes. pp. xliii., 559. Price 3s. 6d.

" Scott," says Heine, " in his every book, gladdens, tranquillizes, and strengthens my heart." This edition contains the whole of Scott's poetical works, with the exception of one or two short poems. While most of Scott's own notes have been retained, others have been added explaining many historical and topographical allusions; and original introductions from the pen of a gentleman familiar with Scotch literature and scenery, containing much interesting information, antiquarian, historical, and biographical, are prefixed to the principal poems. " We can almost sympathise with a middle-aged grumbler, who, after reading Mr. Palgrave's memoir and introduction, should exclaim—' Why was there not such an edition of Scott when I was a schoolboy?'"—GUARDIAN.

Complete Works of Robert Burns.—THE POEMS, SONGS, AND LETTERS, edited from the best Printed and Manuscript Authorities, with Glossarial Index, Notes, and a Biographical Memoir by ALEXANDER SMITH. pp. lxii., 636. Price 3s. 6d.

Burns's poems and songs need not circulate exclusively among Scotchmen, but should be read by all who wish to know the multitudinous capabilities of the Scotch language, and who have the capacity of appreciating the exquisite expression of all kinds of human feeling—rich pawky humour, keen wit, withering satire, genuine pathos, pure passionate love. The exhaustive glossarial index and the copious notes will make all the purely Scotch poems intelligible even to an Englishman. Burns's letters must be read by all who desire fully to appreciate the poet's character, to see it on all its many sides. Explanatory notes are prefixed to most of these letters, and Burns's Journals kept during his Border and Highland Tours, are appended. Following the prefixed biography by the editor, is a Chronological Table of Burns's Life and Works. "Admirable in all respects."—SPECTATOR. "The cheapest, the most perfect, and the most interesting edition which has ever been published."—BELL'S MESSENGER.

Robinson Crusoe. Edited after the Original Editions, with a Biographical Introduction by HENRY KINGSLEY. pp. xxxi., 607. Price 3s. 6d.

Of this matchless truth-like story, it is scarcely possible to find an unabridged edition. This edition may be relied upon as containing the whole of "Robinson Crusoe" as it came from the pen of its author, without mutilation, and with all peculiarities religiously preserved. These points, combined with its handsome paper, large clear type, and moderate price, ought to render this par excellence *the "Globe," the Universal edition of Defoe's fascinating narrative. " A most excellent and in every way desirable edition."*—COURT CIRCULAR. *" Macmillan's ' Globe' Robinson Crusoe is a book to have and to keep."*—MORNING STAR.

Goldsmith's Miscellaneous Works. Edited, with Biographical Introduction, by Professor MASSON. pp. lx., 695. Globe 8vo. 3s. 6d.

This volume comprehends the whole of the prose and poetical works of this most genial of English authors, those only being excluded which are mere compilations. They are all accurately reprinted from the most reliable editions. The faithfulness, fulness, and literary merit of the biography are sufficiently attested by the name of its author, Professor Masson. It contains many interesting anecdotes which will give the reader an insight into Goldsmith's character, and many graphic pictures of the literary life of London during the middle of last century. "Such an admirable compendium of the facts of Goldsmith's life, and so careful and minute a delineation of the mixed traits of his peculiar character as to be a very model of a literary biography in little."—SCOTSMAN.

Pope's Poetical Works. Edited, with Notes and Introductory Memoir, by ADOLPHUS WILLIAM WARD, M.A., Fellow of St. Peter's College, Cambridge, and Professor of History in Owens College, Manchester. pp. lii., 508. Globe 8vo. 3*s.* 6*d.*

This edition contains all Pope's poems, translations, and adaptations, —his now superseded Homeric translations alone being omitted. The text, carefully revised, is taken from the best editions; Pope's own use of capital letters and apostrophised syllables, frequently necessary to an understanding of his meaning, has been preserved; while his uncertain spelling and his frequently perplexing interpunctuation have been judiciously amended. Abundant notes are added, including Pope's own, the best of those of previous editors, and many which are the result of the study and research of the present editor. The introductory Memoir will be found to shed considerable light on the political, social, and literary life of the period in which Pope filled so large a space. The LITERARY CHURCHMAN *remarks: "The editor's own notes and introductory memoir are excellent, the memoir alone would be cheap and well worth buying at the price of the whole volume."*

Dryden's Poetical Works. Edited, with a Memoir, Revised Text, and Notes, by W. D. CHRISTIE, M.A., of Trinity College, Cambridge. pp. lxxxvii., 662. Globe 8vo. 3*s.* 6*d.*

A study of Dryden's works is absolutely necessary to anyone who wishes to understand thoroughly, not only the literature, but also the political and religious history of the eventful period when he lived and reigned as literary dictator. In this edition of his works, which comprises several specimens of his vigorous prose, the text has been thoroughly corrected and purified from many misprints and small changes often materially affecting the sense, which had been allowed to slip in by previous editors. The old spelling has been retained where it is not altogether strange or repulsive. Besides an exhaustive Glossary, there are copious Notes, critical, historical, biographical, and explanatory; and the biography contains the results of considerable original research, which has served to shed light on several hitherto obscure circumstances connected with the life anp parentage of the poet. "An admirable edition, the result of great research and of a careful revision of the text. The memoir prefixed contains, within less than ninety pages, as much sound criticism and as comprehensive a biography as the student of Dryden need desire."—PALL MALL GAZETTE.

Cowper's Poetical Works. Edited, with Notes and Biographical Introduction, by WILLIAM BENHAM, Vicar of Addington and Professor of Modern History in Queen's College, London. pp. lxxiii., 536. Globe 8vo. 3*s.* 6*d.*

This volume contains, arranged under seven heads, the whole of Cowper's own poems, including several never before published, and all his translations except that of Homer's "Iliad." The text is taken from the original editions, and Cowper's own notes are given at the foot of the page, while many explanatory notes by the editor himself are appended to the volume. In the very full Memoir it will be found that much new light has been thrown on some of the most difficult passages of Cowper's spiritually chequered life. "Mr. Benham's edition of Cowper is one of permanent value. The biographical introduction is excellent, full of information, singularly neat and readable and modest—indeed too modest in its comments. The notes are concise and accurate, and the editor has been able to discover and introduce some hitherto unprinted matter. Altogether the book is a very excellent one."—SATURDAY REVIEW.

Morte d'Arthur.—SIR THOMAS MALORY'S BOOK OF KING ARTHUR AND OF HIS NOBLE KNIGHTS OF THE ROUND TABLE. The original Edition of CAXTON, revised for Modern Use. With an Introduction by Sir EDWARD STRACHEY, Bart. pp. xxxvii., 509. Globe 8vo. 3*s.* 6*d.*

This volume contains the cream of the legends of chivalry which have gathered round the shadowy King Arthur and his Knights of the Round Table. Tennyson has drawn largely on them in his cycle of Arthurian Idylls. The language is simple and quaint as that of the Bible, and the many stories of knightly adventure of which the book is made up, are fascinating as those of the "Arabian Nights." The great moral of the book is to " do after the good, and leave the evil." There was a want of an edition of the work at a moderate price, suitable for ordinary readers, and especially for boys: such an edition the present professes to be. The Introduction contains an account of the Origin and Matter of the book, the Text and its several Editions, and an Essay on Chivalry, tracing its history from its origin to its decay. Notes are appended, and a

Glossary of such words as require explanation. "*It is with perfect confidence that we recommend this edition of the old romance to every class of readers.*"—PALL MALL GAZETTE.

The Works of Virgil. Rendered into English Prose, with Introductions, Notes, Running Analysis, and an Index. By JAMES LONSDALE, M.A., late Fellow and Tutor of Balliol College, Oxford, and Classical Professor in King's College, London; and SAMUEL LEE, M.A., Latin Lecturer at University College, London. pp. 288. Price 3s. 6d.

The publishers believe that an accurate and readable translation of all the works of Virgil is perfectly in accordance with the object of the "Globe Library." A new prose-translation has therefore been made by two competent scholars, who have rendered the original faithfully into simple Bible-English, without paraphrase; and at the same time endeavoured to maintain as far as possible the rhythm and majestic flow of the original. On this latter point the DAILY TELEGRAPH *says, "The endeavour to preserve in some degree a rhythm in the prose rendering is almost invariably successful and pleasing in its effect;" and the* EDUCATIONAL TIMES, *that it "may be readily recommended as a model for young students for rendering the poet into English." The General Introduction will be found full of interesting information as to the life of Virgil, the history of opinion concerning his writings, the notions entertained of him during the Middle Ages, editions of his works, his influence on modern poets and on education. To each of his works is prefixed a critical and explanatory introduction, and important aid is afforded to the thorough comprehension of each production by the running Analysis. Appended is an Index of all the proper names and the most important subjects occurring throughout the poems and introductions. "A more complete edition of Virgil in English it is scarcely possible to conceive than the scholarly work before us."* —GLOBE.

www.ingramcontent.com/pod-product-compliance
Lightning Source LLC
Chambersburg PA
CBHW031729230426
43669CB00007B/296